For my good friend
and pahd-ner,
Kevin Royse

[signature]

Hey,
Pahds!

April 11, 1989

Freedom in Jeopardy

Freedom in Jeopardy

Speculations and Observations

*Written and Illustrated by
Edward A. Visser*

VANTAGE PRESS
New York / Los Angeles / Chicago

FIRST EDITION

All rights reserved, including the right of
reproduction in whole or in part in any form.

Copyright © 1989 by Edward A. Visser

Published by Vantage Press, Inc.
516 West 34th Street, New York, New York 10001

Manufactured in the United States of America
ISBN: 0-533-07814-8

Library of Congress Catalog Card No.: 87-90274

To Lou Wojciechowski, Mark and Karen Strobele, Doug Hammond, Brian Schultz, my sister Anne and my brother Mark, Craig Carscallen, Karen Friedman, John Lederer, and everyone else who supported the writing of this book.

The remedy in the United States is not less liberty but real liberty—and end to the brutal intolerence of churchly hooligans and flag-waving corporations and all the rest of the small but bloody despots who have made the word Americanism a synonym for coercion and legal crime.
—Archibald MacLeish
from *The Nation* magazine, December 4, 1937

We do not stand before the government as children before a parent, the government stands before us as the corruptor of our God-given human rights. . . .

—Art Kleps (rev. ed.)
from *Boo Hoo Bible: The Neo-American Church Catechism & Handbook*

Contents

Preface xi

Chapter One. An Introductory Discussion 1
Chapter Two. Propaganda and the Media 14
Chapter Three. Corporate Culture—Adventures in
                         Modern Serfdom 34
Chapter Four. Religion in America—the
                        Simooms of Swindlers 46
Chapter Five. Politics and the Law 63
Chapter Six. Censorship U.S.A. 75
Chapter Seven. Drugs and Alcohol 85
Chapter Eight. A Short Treatise on Iconoclastic
                        Principles 97
Chapter Nine. A Concluding Discussion 102

Preface

My sole purpose in writing this book, as a concerned observer of life in America, is to expose the cultural and constitutional apocalypse that we seem to be heading toward.

For many years, the United States of America, the greatest free nation that has ever existed, has continually set an example for free nations around the world, in the areas of individual rights, and freedom in general.

But nowadays, it seems that the practices and procedures being perpetrated in this country exemplify the things that made Nazi Germany and Soviet Russia great.

It is this writer's contention that we are today faced with some of the most vicious political and corporate criminals that have ever held public office or high position—modern day Hitlers and Mussolinis who are being aided and abetted by other assorted enemies of liberty and justice that intend to turn our country into a police state to satisfy their own selfish attitudes and personal prejudices.

Hopefully, everybody who reads this book will wake up and realize that every individual in this country is in danger, and steps need to be taken immediately to correct this horrendous situation. Otherwise, we will all end up goose-stepping and screaming "Heil Reagan!" with strains of "America Uber Alles" playing in the background. How will we celebrate the 200th anniversary of our Constitution, with a joyful anthem or with an elegy?

March 4, 1789, is the date the Constitution of the United States became the supreme law of the land.[1]

Note the words "supreme law."

Whosoever would tamper with or violate the Constitution

or our Constitutional rights is a lawbreaker of the worst kind—worse than thieves, arsonists, or murderers. Unfortunately, we are currently faced with hordes of self-appointed Constitution-busters from all walks of life, who seem to have forgotten what country this is.

There are still a great many people, however, who hold freedom dear and resent being pushed around.

So, with this in mind, I decided to write this book, and I hope whoever reads it will be comforted in knowing that there are still some people who value highly the U.S. Constitution and personal liberty, and have no intention of letting their lives be ruled by totalitarian phonies and fledgling dictators of all kinds.

The English poet/naturalist Erasmus Darwin (1731–1802) once wrote: "He who allows oppression shares the crime."[2]

It is time for those who cherish freedom to stand up and be counted before we end up having to ask permission just to go to the bathroom.

Enough of this literary appetizer, though—on with the main course.

NOTES

1. Floyd G. Cullop, *The Constitution of the United States: An Introduction* (New York: New American Library, Inc., Mentor Books, 1984), v.
2. George Seldes, *The Great Thoughts* (New York: Ballantine Books, Inc., 1985), 101.

Freedom in Jeopardy

Chapter One
An Introductory Discussion

As we approach the twenty-first century, it has become increasingly apparent that the privacy and sanctity of our personal lives, and our basic rights and freedoms, are being threatened on a regular, daily basis. One by one, our natural liberties to express ourselves freely, to make choices and decisions as we see fit, are being whittled away at an alarming rate. The death of the individual is imminent unless serious steps are taken to combat the tyrannical invasion of our personal lives, and the systematic destruction of our basic freedoms.

There are many causes, reasons, and phenomena that are responsible for this appalling state of affairs that we will examine in detail throughout this book. One of these should be identified at the outset, though, since it is basically one of the major root problems confronting this country.

Most people have heard of Wrestlemania, the current sports fad that has gained such popular acceptance. But how many people are aware of a much more sinister and threatening phenomenon known as Meddlemania, which is characterized by normal, everyday citizens being transmogrified into intolerant meddlers that begin interfering in everything.

Meddlemania is steadily creating an atmosphere of fear, hatred, and intolerance in this country, which has allowed the introduction and passage of repressive and unconstitutional "laws" and programs designed to restrict individual freedom and liberty.

Meddlers seem to be popping out of the woodwork, determined to interfere in every way possible in every thing possible.

It seems as if there is a secret finishing school somewhere that specializes in turning out meddlers and busybodies. Every time you turn around today, someone is sticking his nose into somebody else's business.

Most of this meddling has been instigated by a group of self-righteous hypocrites, a group of people who seem to think of America as their own private country club, and so far as they are concerned, anyone who disagrees with their policies or way of thinking is just more of the "riff-raff" trying to get in the back door. And now they are trying to establish even more club rules.

Sometimes you have to wonder if something hasn't gotten into the nation's water supplies, the way people are running around in a frenzy, passing moral judgments, interfering in other people's lives, attempting to censor this, that, or the other. It's like some kind of epidemic or something.

Every person on the face of the earth should be free. It's bad enough we live in a world where many countries are ruled by repressive, totalitarian regimes; it's even worse to realize that in one of the last strongholds of freedom (this country) we are confronted with self-righteous hypocrites and meddlers who want to perpetuate repressive, intolerant, and unconstitutional laws, practices, values, and beliefs. They are, in effect, the "enemy within," the intellectual termites and spiritual slugs that are eating away at the liberty-oriented structure of this country.

But they don so many masks and disguises that it is sometimes hard to pin them down until you catch them proposing some new repressive, censorship-oriented "moral" program or advocating legislation that restricts or punishes other individuals. And inevitably, they surface sooner or later because the urge to meddle and interfere becomes intoxicating and overpowering, kind of like a mental case of poison ivy. One of the most invidious schemes the Meddlemaniacs have come up with lately is the the blood and urine testing programs that are currently being perpetrated on the public.

The removal of one's body fluids to test for "wrongdoing" is such a gross violation of one's person and freedoms that there are scarcely words to describe the kind of vulgar and shameless mentality that could dream up such a vicious plot.

Obviously, the miscreants in Washington, D.C., and corporate boardrooms have been rereading "Mein Kampf" and have been brushing up on totalitarian techniques. The Russians and Red Chinese must be vigorously applauding the institution of these testing programs; no doubt they must think American "leaders" have come around to their way of thinking. The biggest offenders behind these programs (after the Federal government) are large corporations, whose directors and owners have become so greedy and self-righteous, they have lost all respect and consideration where the rights and liberties of their employees are concerned.

The employer-employee relationship is a two-way street; if every worker in the country walked off the job for just one day, the corporate dictators would lose hundreds of millions of dollars and would be forced to step back in line and back off. It would seem that these pompous businessmen are going too far and pushing their luck by interfering and meddling in the lives of their employees, the people who make money for them and to whom they should be grateful. An excerpt from a letter that I wrote to *Time* magazine concerning an article in their March 17, 1986 issue sort of sums up the situation:

> Dear Mr. Editor,
> I am shocked that *Time* magazine would present such a slanted, biased article such as your March 17 'Drugs On The Job' piece. The blood and urine testing program is one of the most vicious assaults ever launched against individual freedom and liberty. What comes after this? Spot checks on our underwear to make sure they are clean and unstained, with mandatory jail sentences for those with dirty shorts?
> Millions of decent, hardworking Americans enjoy using drugs in the privacy of their own homes and should have every right to. Obviously, even if you abstain at work traces would show up in a random test and could be used against you, even though it's nobody's business but your own. These Nazi-style tactics are the products of a group of self-righteous, hypocritical meddlers who think they can

buy a seat in Heaven by enforcing their morality on others and interfering in their personal lives.

It's nobody else's business if a person drinks beer or smokes pot, any more than if they wear blue shoes, eat tuna fish, or anything else. After all, were the Pilgrims or cowboys and Indians strip-searched or was their urine tested?

The beginning of the Fourth Amendment of the Constitution of the United States reads as follows: "The right of the people to be secure [safe] in their persons, houses, papers, and effects [other personal property], against unreasonable searches or seizures [arrest or taking of belongings] shall not be violated. . . ."

Warrants (written court orders) for any of these purposes must be issued with good cause and sworn to by oath and must describe in detail the place to be searched and the persons or things to be seized. This protects persons from "writs of assistance" (general warrants allowing any search or seizure anytime anyplace) such as were used by the British.[1]

Anyone with half a brain should be able to see that these testing programs clearly fall under the heading of "writs of assistance" and are obviously in violation of the Constitution and are unacceptable. They fall under the heading of "writs of assistance" because they are supposed to be random tests inflicted on the general population whenever some meddling troublemaker decides to indulge in a little constitution-busting. These testing programs are the result of a self-righteous, intolerant mentality that will allow no opposition, and are clear indicators of another witch-hunt in which a majority of innocent people will suffer. What a person does on his own time is his own business and concerns no one else.

Admittedly, any employee who is habitually late or absent, who causes trouble or accidents, or who is guilty of constant bad workmanship could possibly be suspected of having an alcohol or drug problem, and maybe should be confronted. But no employee who performs his duties as required and abstains from alcohol or drug use on the job should be penalized for their off-duty activities.

All this antidrug witch-hunt fever is producing devastating results. Every time an accident occurs or someone calls in sick to work, the first thing the meddlers want to do is yank down the offender's shorts and get a urine sample so they can convict him or her of "wrongdoing."

According to the August 11, 1986 broadcast of the "Independent Network News," the meddlers have attempted to introduce an even more obscene wrinkle to testing proceedings.

Not only do they want to sample every citizen's urine; they also want witnesses or examiners to watch each victim urinate in a sample cup, to make sure they don't substitute "clean" urine for their own or put neutralizing chemicals in their urine to get a negative test result. This is clearly a vulgar and despicable trespass against the privacy and dignity of every person subjected to it.

How can a free people tolerate such vile and base indecencies? You would think that any time a person is forced to piss in a cup he would feel soiled and degraded and would deeply resent such a vile indignity.

But millions of Americans let themselves be pushed around every day even though these practices are clearly unconstitutional, ruthless, and immoral. They violate the integrity, rights, and person of every American citizen.

They are also partially in violation of the Fifth Amendment. If you know you have drugs or alcohol in your system and submit to urinalysis, you are knowingly incriminating yourself. If you refuse to be tested, this appears just as incriminating. It's a catch-22 situation where each individual gets the short end of the stick no matter what. Not only are the Fourth and Fifth Amendments being compromised, the Ninth Amendment is taking a licking, too. The Ninth Amendment states the enumeration of certain rights in the Constitution does not mean these are the only rights the people have. To list all the many rights the people of the United States simply take for granted would be impossible, but every citizen should be aware that he has these rights in order to protect them. Presumably, this means that U.S. citizens have the right to live in a meddler-free environ-

DR. STRANGEPISS

ment, safe from the excesses of government snoopers, urine testers, and storm troopers. Another outrageous example of self-righteous aggression is the recent boycotting and picketing of 7-11 stores by members of the bafflingly named Moral Majority, which resulted in the mighty Southland Corporation buckling at the knees and agreeing not to sell adult magazines in any of their stores. Of course, I can't seem to remember any press releases indicating that Jerry Falwell had been elevated to godhood, but it seems that many stupid and naïve individuals regard him as supreme judge and are ready to meddle upon his command.

And who can forget the cynical, heavy-handed enactment of seat belt laws in many states where no public vote was held to decide if the citizenry wanted to be forced to wear seat belts?

This "law" was supposedly created to protect and save lives, but when one remembers the fifty-dollar fine (at least in New York State) for getting caught not wearing a seat belt, it is easy to see that this is just another scheme to rake in cash and police the public. (Earlier in the year, "Adolf" Reagan threatened to withhold federal highway funds from any state that refused to enact mandatory seat belt laws.) To back up this act of aggression, the government actively bombards the public with celebrity-endorsed TV spots that advocate the use of seat belts and remind everybody that it's "the law." This ominous phrase is heavily used nowadays on a variety of so-called "public service" spots, from Selective Service to child support programs, and is indicative of a growing trend toward dictatorial authoritarianism among our elected officials, the people who are supposed to serve the public instead of trying to police and dominate it.

It seems totally wrong for the taxpayers of this country to pay the salaries of these politicians when, instead of tending to the business of running the government and the myriad of government agencies that raise our tax dollars, they spend their time interfering in our personal lives and sermonizing on so-called "moral" issues. The necessity and purpose of government in a free society should be for the practical administration of needed functions: highway building and maintenance; public works facilities such as water works, sewer, and waste management; public services such as senior citizen housing, et cetera.

When government officials begin meddling and interfering with the everyday lives and rights of the people, we are looking at outright acts of tyranny and aggression.

Lines should be clearly drawn here. Are we paying these people for their services as officials and executors of government functions, or are we paying them to dictate morality and chaperone us? If the latter is true, I want a refund.

The ironic part is that while these self-righteous boobs are standing on their soap boxes, preaching "morality" and spewing right wing nonsequiturs and double-talk, the United States Government continues to be one of the most costly, inefficient, bumbling organizations on the face of the earth. If these politicians spent as much time trying to manage and run the government as they do dreaming up pseudo-ideology and morality, we would all be much the better for it. Maybe what we need is a special politician school where bureaucrats are taught how to run the affairs of government agencies and are trained to avoid meddling in other people's affairs.

But the problem is much more complicated than that.

It would seem that a conspiracy has been instigated by a coalition of self-righteous politicians, right-wing pressure groups, "religious" organizations and "religious" leaders, corporate executives, and various fascistic infiltration/action groups, all acting together in concert.

And it would seem obvious from their actions and the unconstitutional practices they are trying to shove down America's throat that they have totally forgotten that this is the United States, not the Soviet Union, that this is the land of the free and the home of the brave, not the land of the oppressed and the home of the slave.

It never seems to occur to any of these dolts that maybe the vast majority of people in this country would rather be left alone to do their own thing and live their own lives without any outside interference. And even if it does, a heavy-duty case of Meddlemania or the Snoopy Sniffer Syndrome seems to set in immediately, and they justify their interference by implying that they are morally superior to others and possess some kind of divine right to meddle and dictate morality.

The Snoopy Sniffer Syndrome is what happens to a Meddlemaniac who becomes overly obsessed with meddling and goes off the deep end. A Snoopy Sniffer spends every waking moment sticking his nose into somebody else's business.

They become so devoted to interfering and meddling that there is just no reasoning or talking to them. More than likely these people could use a couple of months on a psychiatrist's couch, although I'm not sure there is a cure for Meddlemania or the Snoopy Sniffer Syndrome.

This immoral and tyrannical policing of America has reached epidemic proportions, and all adults and free-thinking individuals should resent the presumptuous and high-handed attitude of government and right-wing pressure groups like the Moral (?) Majority, who have the audacity to treat the public like naughty children.

Another occurrence foreshadowing totalitarian practices in America is the appointment of William H. Rehnquist as Chief Justice of the United States Supreme Court, who, according to the June 18, 1986, edition of the CBS Early Morning News, supports more police authority in dealing with suspects (yipes! Could this be the end of *Miranda-Escobedo*? Don't we really need more restraint over the police?) and who also supports more government secrecy. (This is unacceptable. We have already seen what kind of swinish activities go on when the government isn't kept under close scrutiny from the Teapot Dome Scandal in the early 1900s up to Watergate and the Iranian-Contra situation of the present. How many wars and military actions have we become involved in for geo-political reasons known only to a few?).

The truths and principles in the United States Constitution and Bill of Rights are supposed to be clear-cut and self-evident so that even the simplest citizen understands what he or she is entitled to without a lot of nebulous, murky legal "deciphering."

Nowadays, though, we see the constant perversion and distortion of our constitutional rights by black-robed judges and

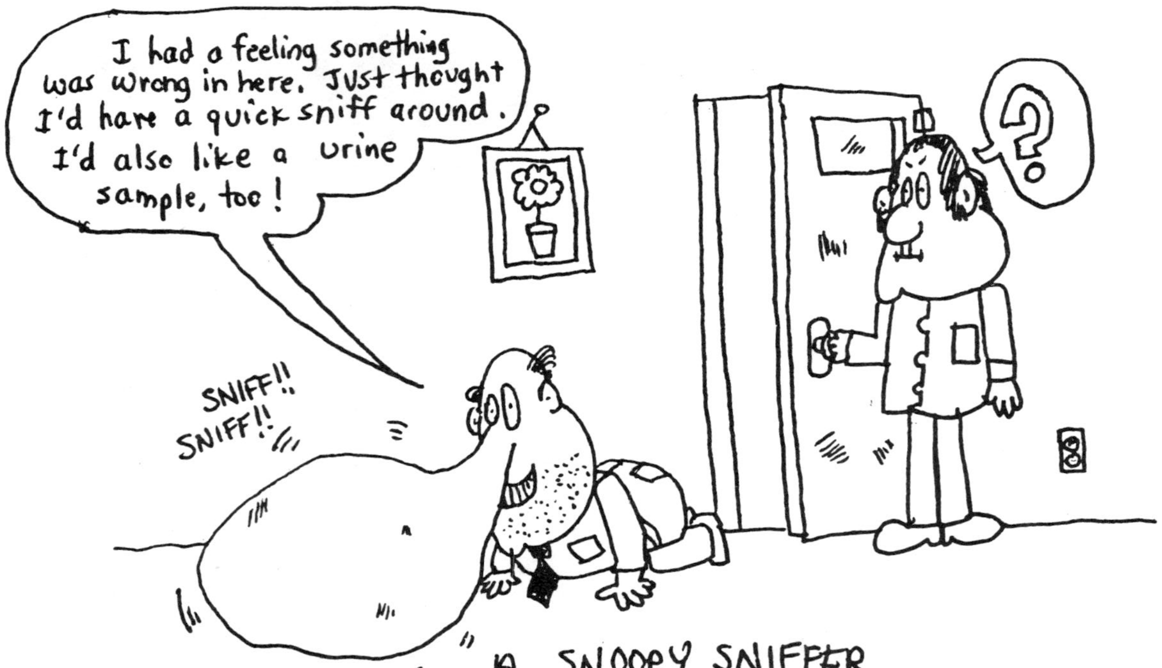

A SNOOPY SNIFFER IN ACTION

legal "experts," who write ten or twenty page opinions "explaining" why unconstitutional practices can all of a sudden be constitutional, and vice versa, so they can please their political godfathers and patrons. This judicial puppet show has become such a farce, you have to wonder how these justices can keep a straight face when they hand down unconstitutional decisions that they know infringe on the rights of the American public.

There is a certain psychology behind all these invasions of our privacy and the circumcision of our freedoms.

The idea is if someone is always afraid of breaking some "law" and is worried about it, then he is more easily controlled and intimidated and turned into a puppet.

If you continually invade more privacy and trample on more freedoms and bombard the public with all kinds of media spots that feature policemen, the sound of a slamming jail door, and the words or letters saying "it's the law," then more than likely most people will live in a constant state of apprehension and subservience, not knowing if a couple of storm troopers are going to kick in the front door at midnight and haul them off to a cell somewhere. The government and its puppet media have distorted the word patriotism and twisted it around to mean mindless submission to the government machine and society. They have employed Orwellian "newspeak" so often that most people seem to be foundering in a maelstrom of semantic confusion, which explains why so many members of the public seem to be unaware of just how badly we are being ripped off.

You would think that the American public would get tired of being slapped around and intimidated by the buffoons in power, but it is easy to see why they don't when you look around and see the population drowning in all the snake oil that has already been poured out.

This snake oil, commonly known as propaganda, is being dispensed in such a powerful, unending stream that most people have a hard time just treading water, let alone swimming upstream.

The national situation could be compared to a real-life, on-running episode of the "Dukes of Hazzard," with plenty of Boss

Hogg's and Sheriff Roscoes attempting to bamboozle and rip off the public at every turn. In the following chapters, we will attempt to consider and analyze these threats to our freedom and understand the underlying reasons for them.

To finish this chapter, we will conclude with another occurrence pointing toward a conspiracy to police America.

Several months after the 7-11/Moral Majority episode went down, out came "The Meese Commission's Report on Pornography," which, among other things, recommends citizens to use the same self-righteous techniques (boycotting, picketing, et cetera) in their communities that the Moral Majority used on the Southland Corporation.

In an article in the September 1986 issue of *Forum* magazine entitled "A Magna Carta For Censors," Eric Nadler and Philip Nobile reveal that "under the flimsy guise of 'educating' the public, the commission approved a how-to-protest manual which mentioned boycotts of porn retailers and the support of corporations that use their power 'responsibly' (i.e., don't do business with peddlers of offenseive material)."

Lately, we seem to be plagued by presidential "commissions" that are involving themselves in areas that are none of their business. Instead of conducting studies that deal with important problems like inflation, unemployment, wasteful government spending, and a host of other serious affairs, they serve up self-serving propaganda that promotes their 'moral' values and ideological viewpoints. If this doesn't sound like a Meddlemania conspiracy, I don't know what would.

One has to wonder how much the Reagan Administration and the Moral Majority spent out of their censorship slush fund to have the "report" conjured up.

Admittedly, some porn is repulsive (such as kiddie porn). But where does the line get drawn, and who gets to draw it?

NOZEE
Meddler Academy
DIAL 1-800-MEDDLER

Some people will take a mile if given an inch, and since it seems that the "moral" pressure groups want to sterilize America to their liking, should they be allowed to dictate status quo morality for the entire nation?

NOTE

1. Floyd G. Cullop, *The Consitituion of the United States: An Introduction*, 75.

Chapter Two
Propaganda and the Media

To understand why all this meddling and interference is possible, and what the root causes are, we have to look back into the past.

As Ovid Demaris noted, America has always suffered from "historical amnesia"[1] about itself, and the media has done little to cure the problem.

Despite the glamorization of the Pilgrims and the founding fathers of this country in history books and in countless TV shows, mini-series, and movies, the true facts are quite different from the candy-coated lies that we have been led to believe.

Real American history is rife with examples of bigotry, racial and religious intolerance and persecution, the wanton destruction of individual lives by ridiculous and repressive "laws" and crusades (from the Salem witch-hunts up to modern drug testing programs), and a great deal of foundationless prejudices.

Several pages from Mr. Demaris's book, *America the Violent*, help to illustrate the way things started out in this country, contrary to popular mythology, with many parallels into the present day.

> So violence from religious bigotry had come to America as had violence from racial bigotry. Both were to remain, to be compounded by the smug self-satisfaction of the Pilgrims—the "only true Christians in all the world," as their Reverend John Smyth described them. But in the words of Gustavus Myers in his *History of Bigotry in the United States*, they took with them to America "Old World ideas of proscription by force of which the established religion or creed

aimed to enforce its code of doctrines and assure its supremacy." Of the 102 passengers cramped on board the *Mayflower*, only forty-one were Pilgrims in any sense of the word. The great majority were "strangers," mostly members in more or less good standing of the Church of England who were going to the New World not to practice their religion but simply to make better lives for themselves. In the opinion of Christopher Martin, the Pilgrims were a "forwarde and waspish, discontented people. . . . "

The opinion of the crew of the *Mayflower* was unprintable. They had come to hate the Pilgrims so much that they were "cursing them daily with greevous execrations." Only the kindliness of the captain and the first mate and the courage of the other officers seem to have kept the crew from attacking the "saints" bodily. Mutiny broke out on the *Mayflower* when the "strangers" came to understand that the contracts they had signed placed them under the rule of the "saints" and that the Pilgrims determined to, as Willison puts it in *Saints and Strangers*, "impose their religious views upon the majority whether the latter chose to accept the Holy Discipline or not."

The Mayflower Compact has been hailed as a cornerstone of American freedom, but it was actually intended, Willison points out, to "maintain the status quo on the *Mayflower*, to show inferiors in general and servants in particular their place and keep them where they belonged—i.e., under the thumbs of their masters."

"American democracy was not born in the cabin of the *Mayflower*," says historian Samuel Eliot Morison.

Violence broke out soon after the first landing at Plymouth when the Pilgrims desecrated Indian burial grounds, stole their buried grain and other food supplies, and, led by Captain Myles Standish, also known as "Captain Shrimpe," chased a group of six Indians through the woods.[2]

Well, it would certainly seem that things were off to a rip-roaring start in this country, what with Captain Shrimpe and the rest of the haughty hypocrites imposing their beliefs on their fellow shipmates, and attacking, robbing, and killing the Indians.

It sort of sounds like intolerance and self-righteous aggression have been with us for quite a while, doesn't it?

We can see modern-day codes of doctrines and viewpoints being imposed by "proscription by force" in the form of seat belt "laws," drug testing programs, the attempts by the Meese Commission and the moral majority to ban pornography, and other assorted items such as the banning of smoking in many public places through the efforts of pressure groups.

Quoting again from Mr. Demaris's book in a section that illustrates the futility and immorality of any type of witch-hunt, we find that "The Puritans, almost out of Indians to kill, now turned to hanging witches."

The phenomenon started in Salem with a group of young girls and a West Indian slave woman, Tituba, who was fond of telling ghost stories. Before it was over, nineteen people had been hanged, one "witch" pressed to death, and some two hundred thrown into jail.

Previously, New England and the rest of the colonies had been singularly free of the witchcraftmania that was sweeping Old England and all of Europe.

But in 1681, a group of clergymen, led by Increase Mather, had taken it upon themselves to combat the danger to religion with proof of the supernatural.

So they gathered and set down every instance they could discover of "divine judgments, tempests, floods, earthquakes, thunders as are unusual, strange apparitions, or whatever else shall happen that is prodigious, witchcrafts, diabolical possessions, remarkable judgments upon noted sinners, eminent deliverances and answers to prayer."

"Hangman, do your duty!" was an everyday verdict, and another witch was duly carted off and hanged.

The trials and hangings might have gone on indefinitely if the accusers had not made a mistake or two.

They accused the wife of one of the most virulent of the witch-hunters, the Rev. John Hale, of being a witch. The minister suddenly changed his mind about the whole matter and denounced the trials as nothing but superstition.[3]

Quite an embarrassing episode, wouldn't you say? Innocent men and women killed or incarcerated because of the superstitious prejudices and self-righteous attitudes of a few.

This isn't usually elaborated on much in most so-called "history" books. But if you look back at the way American history really is, it is easy to see that it has almost always been a case of one faction and ideology versus another, with one side almost inevitably getting hurt (remember the Civil War?).

People forget this reality, however, and this helps to keep up the myth that has been passed down from one generation and administration to another, that Americans have always been the valiant soldiers of righteousness, and that America has always been a citadel of liberty and truth, despite the facts that point otherwise, in other words, to keep alive a spirit of "nationalism" that can be used to manipulate the masses emotionally, spiritually and intellectually.

Obviously, it would definitely come as a surprise to the nation that we were getting involved in some kind of conflict, or that we were having some governmental trespass inflicted on us if it hadn't already been introduced to the public in stages as a "problem," and carefully built up by keeping constant attention focused on the situation via the news media, with plenty of "experts" and politicians advocating and expounding on the rightness of the government position. Adolf Hitler and his cronies made extensive use of what mass media existed during their time (newsreels, movies, newspapers, and radio) for every purpose imaginable, and proved beyond a shadow of a doubt what kind of hypnotic and devastating effects a well-organized propaganda campaign can produce.

Nowadays in this country, everybody from the government on down to the most ridiculous pressure groups are using the media, especially television, to promote their preposterous ideas and viewpoints. Issues get more trivial and petty; people are ready to jump on the nearest bandwagon at the drop of a hat and start a campaign to outlaw or ban something.

And before you know it, some self-appointed "expert" is appearing on TV, spouting half-baked drivel in an attempt to swing public opinion in his direction.

Hitler's explanation for the use of propaganda was: "There is only so much room in a brain, so much wall space as it were, and if you furnish it with your slogans, the opposition has no place to put up any pictures later on, because the apartment of the brain is already crowded with your furniture."[4]

It should be clear that this theory is constantly put into practice every day, in many ways, and by a wide variety of perpetrators.

A prime example of a current propaganda campaign that has been manufactured by the media in cahoots with the government (with all the earmarks of a modern-day Inquisition/witch-hunt) is the so-called "war on drugs."

This "war" is really a war on individual freedom of choice, the Fourth Amendment, and a large section of the U.S. population—a "war" that displays Pilgrimish attitudes of intolerance and self-righteous prudishness. The real reasons for the "war" will be discussed in a later chapter.

This tyrannical act of aggression is the result of a collection of vicious lies and misinformation known as "The Report by the President's Commission on Organized Crime," which, among other outrages, recommends victimizing the American public with urine testing and the recriminalization of marijuana.

You have to wonder how anyone born in this country could think it was right in any way to violate the Constitution or foist totalitarian practices on the sovereign citizens of this great nation.

Since all this nonsense started in early 1986, hardly a day has gone by without some sort of antidrug propaganda being spewed out by the media.

From news programs to daytime soap operas, from celebrity-endorsed "Stop the Madness" media spots to prime time detective shows, practically everywhere you turn, some sort of exaggerated anti-drug rhetoric is being perpetuated in all-out effort to deceive and brainwash the American public.

Now, the Reagan Administration has openly admitted that they plan to use all kinds of media propaganda in the "war on drugs," regardless of whether the whole campaign is a trespass against the American public or not.

Kevin Zeese, national director of NORML (the National Organization for the Reform of Marijuana Laws) estimates that there are thirty million marijuana users in the U.S.A. This is more than the combined populations of the states of Iowa, Mississippi, Nebraska, Kansas, Connecticut, Colorado, Arizona, and Illinois. Most of these people are hard-working professionals and responsible adults, who pay their taxes and see nothing wrong or immoral with smoking an occasional joint. Does this matter to the Meddlemaniacs or the Snoopy Sniffers? Of course not!

They have escalated their assaults even more, using the hard-earned tax dollars of many NORML members to destroy more marijuana crops and stop incoming drug shipments.

According to the August 15, 1986 edition of the "CBS Early Morning News," Attorney General Edwin Meese wanted to waste $266 million of our tax money to provide 550 drug agents and surveillance planes to patrol the Mexican border.

Obviously, this governmental interference and meddling wouldn't have reached such outrageous proportions if it hadn't been aided and abetted by the media, especially television.

What every citizen in this country should remember is that news programs have become the biggest offenders in this respect. Whether national or local, by promoting a despicable and unconstitutional practice like urine testing, they have consciously attempted to sell the public a lie and have tried to make police state tactics seem acceptable.

News programs have become more and more one-sided, with a tendency to advocate governmental intrusion and aggression, while they deny the validity and supremacy of the individual, individual rights, and constitutional freedoms.

Who needs all this constant "news," anyhow?

These daily news programs and hourly updates have created a synthetic "stream of consciousness" in the collective public mind, into which are constantly injected the attitudes and opinions of authority figures and so-called "experts" that produce dogmatic, Pavlovian responses in people.

The hysteria stirred up by the media and the meddlers with

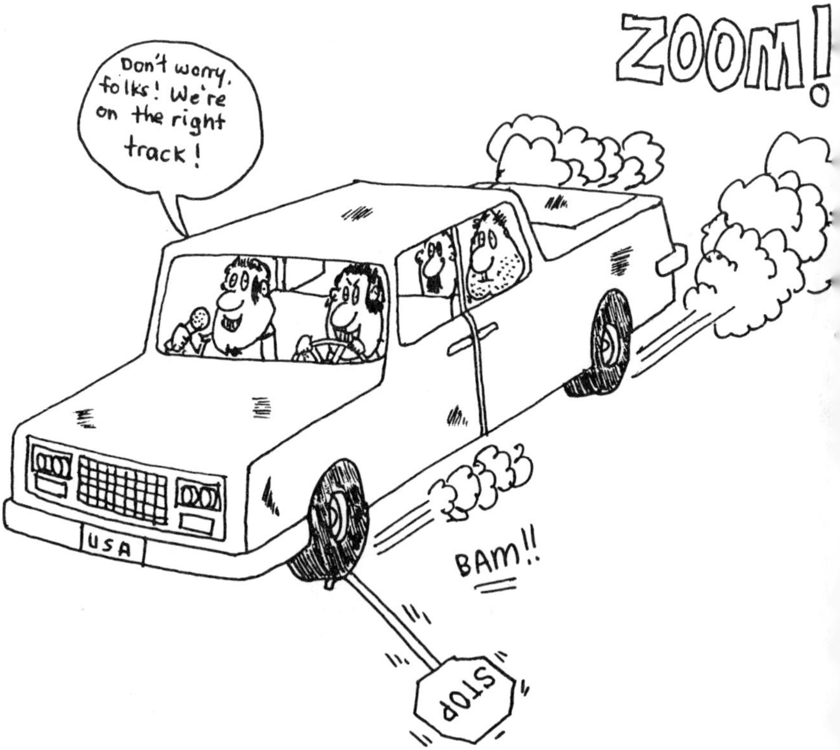
Don't worry, folks! We're on the right track!
ZOOM!
USA
BAM!!
STOP

the "war on drugs" could be compared to someone seeing a cigar smoldering in an ashtray on the ground floor of a ten-story hotel, and screaming, "Fire!" and pulling all the alarms, and getting the entire building in an uproar.

On September 2, 1986, CBS News and the *New York Times* released the results of a poll that showed that in April, 1986 only 2 percent of the people surveyed thought that drugs were a problem. Then, a bare four months later, 13 percent of the people surveyed thought that drugs were the number one problem in the country. Now, all this antidrug nonsense didn't start becoming such a big deal until January 1986, so it should be easy to see that in just a short time the public consciousness can be massaged and manipulated into believing anything through the relentless flow of propaganda via the media.

This intense, everyday bombardment of antidrug propaganda and misinformation illustrates more Hitlerian concepts about media compaigning:

> Never concede that there may be some good in your enemy; never leave room for alternatives; never accept blame; concentrate on one enemy at a time and blame him for everything that goes wrong; people will believe a big lie sooner than a small one; and if you repeat it frequently enough people will believe it sooner or later.[5]

And all the lies and fables that they have disseminated have caused an even uglier phenomenon than the urine testing programs (if that could be possible).

Something one would have thought would have died in Nazi Germany or would at least be confined to the Communist Bloc has reared its ugly head—children betraying their parents to the police.

A story in the August 15, 1986 edition of the *USA Today* newspaper, written by Lynne Jankowski, states that thirteen-year-old Deanna Young of Tustin, California, turned her parents in to police for drug possession after being brainwashed by antidrug propaganda at a local church.

MEDIA PROPAGANDA OVERDOSE

Of course, *USA Today* totally supported the government position, did nothing to point out how despicable it is for a child to turn his or her parents in to the police, and even printed a quotation from archmeddler Nancy Reagan herself, who said that she thought Deanna must have loved her parents a great deal to do something like that! What comes after this? Schoolchildren turned into conniving, untrustworthy little monsters, ready to turn in other family members for anything? Parents and relatives turned in for harboring libertarian or leftwing sympathies?

For a while, Deanna was in a state shelter for children, and her parents were in custody and facing ten years in the pokey, and for what?

This was a family nearly destroyed by irresponsible propaganda. After the whole thing blew over (when Mr. and Mrs. Young agreed to enter drug "rehabilitation" programs), they turned down (congratulations!) an offer to make a TV movie about the whole episode, a movie that no doubt would have depicted a young child's struggle of conscience (probably with plenty of violin music in the background), with the kid deciding to do the "right" thing by informing the police. No doubt, it would have been a touching piece of propaganda. This kangaroo-court approach to drug controls should be an affront to every American, and it is shameful to see that hardly any legislators, judges, or other public officials have the guts to stand up and condemn this black farce for the unconstitutional and un-American fraud that it is.

There is one exception that deserves to be mentioned. On Wednesday, November 12, 1986, U.S. District Court Judge Robert Collins of New Orleans ordered the Customs Service to stop testing their employees' urine for drugs, calling the practice unconstitutional. In Justice Collins's words: "The drug testing program is a degrading procedure that so detracts from human dignity and self-respect that it shocks the conscience and offends this court's sense of justice."[6]

I would like to applaud this constitutional patriot for his honor and lucidity, two qualities that seem to be rare these days.

Why does the public allow this to go on? Why have they

been misled so badly? Most of it is due to the fact that they have been bamboozled by a battery of "experts," and these "experts" aren't worth the paper they're printed on, in many cases.

In his book *Looking Out for Number One*, Robert J. Ringer exposes the expert myth with a real-life example:

> A director and an instructor in psychiatry, both from the University of Southern California medical school, teamed with an assistant professor of medical education at Southern Illinois University to conduct a rather unusual experiment.
>
> They arranged to have a Dr. Myron L. Fox, purportedly an authority on the application of mathematics to human behavior, speak to a group of fifty-five educators, school administrators, psychiatrists, psychologists and social workers. His topic was "mathematical game theory as applied to physician education."
>
> It must have been a great speech, because forty-two of the fifty-five in attendance commented that the speaker's examples helped clarify the subject and that the material was well organized and the lecture stimulating.
>
> All of this was fine, except for one small matter: "Dr. Fox" was a hired actor and his "lecture" was never meant to be anything but pure double-talk.[7]

After digesting this exposé, it should be easy to see that most of the so-called "experts" who back up and advocate the extremist aggression originating in the White House, on every subject from drug testing programs to military intervention in Nicaragua and Grenada up to forced nationwide adoption of seat belt laws are nothing more than the puppet mouthpieces— the "ventriloquist's dummies" if you will—who simply serve as window dressing to cast all this authoritarian terrorism in an acceptable light.

If you were to take Mr. Ringer's exposé and expand on it exponentially, it would probably give you goose bumps all over at the thought of how many charlatans and fakers are out there conning the public and convincing them to accept a lot of nonsensical ideas and programs.

To illustrate in a simple, nutshell way how the media and "experts" operate to pull the wool over the public's eyes, just picture this nation as an automobile, with whatever administration is in power representing the driver, the passengers in the backseat representing the public, the fuel in the gas tank representing our tax dollars, and the passengers in the front seat representing the news media and "experts".

Then picture the car careening wildly out of control, speeding down the road, burning up lots of precious fuel—while the front seat passengers (the news media and "experts") keep on reassuring the passengers in the backseat (the public) that everything is all right and the car (our nation) is on the right course. Get the picture?

It seems that every time a new administration takes office, they want to go for a joyride and burn up fuel like its going out of style. And it would seem that the Reagan Administration delights in taking all kinds of side roads and back routes, regardless of what kind of damage might befall the car.

Today, on most news programs, anyone who disagrees with the folly being perpetrated in Washington, D.C., is portrayed as a malcontent or a misguided dissident, and the "good, patriotic" people are those who have blind faith in our glorious leaders and subserviently obey whatever "laws" or policies that are drafted, no matter how stupid or ridiculous they might be.

And, of course, the media has a tendency to glorify government officials, especially the president, almost to the point of deification. This explains why most of the public will swallow almost anything that they are told in a presidential address or "fireside chat," and accept it as gospel truth.

In a constitutional country like the United States, all government officials from the president on down are supposed to be the servants of the people, not the rulers. When they try taking over and ruling and the people go along with it, we end up faced with a situation that Dr. Carl Jung warned of when he wrote:

> The State in particular is turned into a quasi-animate personality from whom everything is expected. In reality it is only a camouflage for those individuals who know how to manipulate it. Thus the constitutional State drifts into the situation of a primitive form of society, namely the communism of a primitive tribe where everybody is subject to the autocratic rule of a chief or an oligarchy.[8]

In other words, whenever a majority of the population starts depending on "authority figures" and government leaders to provide direction in all matters and establish "moral" policy, the door opens up for every would-be dictator and meddler in the business. And before you know it, a small handful of people who, unfortunately, have the powers of the police, the military, the courts, and the law behind them, end up being able to enforce whatever policies or legislation they desire upon the vast majority.

I think it appropriate here to quote the German philosopher Friedrich Nietzsche:

> And others are proud of their handful of righteousness and for its sake commit wanton outrage upon all things: so that the world is drowned in their unrighteousness. Alas, how ill the word 'virtue' sounds in their mouths! And when they say: "I am just," it always sounds like: "I am revenged!"
>
> They want to scratch out the eyes of their enemies with their virtue; and they raise themselves only in order to lower others.[9]

The situation today seems reminiscent of some kind of episode you could expect to see on "Star Trek," where some strange virus takes ahold of the crew of the bridge (the government) and they start victimizing the rest of the crew (the public) and begin to do a lot of strange things.

Most people have gotten so used to being mindlessly obedient to authority, they wouldn't know totalitarianism if it slapped them in the face. This explains why there has been such a lack of public outrage over things like the "great urine testing swindle." Let's face it: you can call someone an expletive to his face, and if you say it in a certain way, he'll think he is being complimented.

In the same way, the news media presents different issues in ways that make them look truthful and correct, even though they might be preposterous and fraudulent.

All politicians are human; they have to eat, sleep, and go to the bathroom just like anyone else. They seem to forget this, however, once they get into office and the media begin their glorification processes.

Probably the best thing we could do is make it a requirement that each office occupied by a government official have the following lines, composed by the Japanese poet/philosopher Bassho, hung up in a conspicuous place at all times: "A reasonable number of fleas is good for a dog. Otherwise the dog forgets he is a dog." Obviously, many politicians and "moral" crusaders are sadly lacking in the flea department, and as a result, their britches are bursting at the seams, and they will stop at nothing in their ruthless, self-righteous drive to impose their values and beliefs on the public at large.

It should be clear that just about anybody can be made to believe anything if he is bombarded over and over again with the same propaganda. And it helps if someone the public supposedly trusts is doing the propagandizing.

For example, media puppet Geraldo Rivera, who bored television viewers with his farcical, pseudodocumentary on Al Capone's vaults in 1986 has decided to jump on the drug bandwagon.

According to the November 29–December 5, 1986 issue of *TV Guide*, Rivera's latest farce, "American Vice: The Doping of a Nation," will not only trace the cocaine path from South America to the U.S., but it will also feature (wow!) a live drug bust. According to the article, written by Elaine Warren:

> After months of research, Rivera says he's sure that the war on drugs will never be won by attacking the suppliers only. If the approach to the drug problem in the United States continues to be the supply-side approach, then attempts to solve the drug crisis are a lost cause.
>
> We need to address the demand side. Rivera, an advocate of drug testing, says he will take a drug test himself on the air.[10]

Spoken like a true aider and abettor of the constitution-busting criminals in government office. If "comrade" Rivera wants to promote unconstitutional practices and interfere with the freedom of choice of others, then maybe he should take a job as a broadcaster in East Germany or Albania.

Another quotation from Hitler reads "Words build bridges into unexplored regions."[11]

An example of this (in the propaganda sense) is the way that "education" and "rehabilitation" is recommended for anyone discovered to be using drugs.

Despite the fact that millions of people enjoy using drugs and don't feel that they have a problem, in many cases they get railroaded into "treatment" programs and end up having their intelligence insulted by "experts" who deliver a lot of double-talk and outright nonsense under the heading of "education," and are blackmailed into abstaining from practices that they enjoy on their own time, under the threat of losing their jobs or being thrown into jail ("rehabilitation").

In other words, it's another exercise in pseudosemantics, as drug use is condemned over and over again as being unhealthy, immoral, and dangerous by endless words in newspaper articles and constant verbal testimonies from "experts," and million of gullible Americans believe all this because they have been bludgeoned by endless batteries of fables, doctrines, and cleverly worded "information" that they have come to accept as "truth."

When was the last time you saw a member of NORML or a private citizen defending the smoking of marijuana? When was the last time you saw anyone condemning seat belt laws as the act of a Big Brother mentality? How often do you see anyone condemning the laboratory testing of human excrement to condemn and incriminate individuals everywhere?

It definitely looks like the media has been told to play along with all this, or else.

And in all their fervent zeal and enthusiasm, they seem to be forgetting that they are helping to tighten the noose.

And, as far as seat belts go, this mandatory "buckling up" is just the kind of cretinous scheme one might expect nowadays. Maybe seat belts save lives in some cases.

But what about a situation where an accident occurs, the car starts on fire, the seat belt won't unlock, and there are no shears or knife handy to cut through it?

I personally was in the front seat of a car with two friends of mine, and we were cut off, and the guy driving drove off the road and straight into a telephone pole, totaling the car.

All three of us walked away from the crash with minor injuries (bruises on foreheads and knees), and none of us were wearing seat belts.

If one person ends up getting killed because he was wearing a seat belt and couldn't get loose in a dangerous situation (presuming that he was "buckled up" because it was the "law"), then this "law" would be in partial violation of the Fourteenth Amendment, which states in the second paragraph of Section One:

> No state can make laws that abridge [take away or restrict] any right, privelege, or protection of citizens of the United States; nor pass laws that may cost a person his life, imprison him, or fine him, unless he had been found guilty of a crime in a court of law by due process of law [following fair legal practices based upon fair laws].[12]

This whole seat belt scam has also been heavily promoted by the media, most notably in the form of the absurd "test dummy" spots.

Of course, every effort to promote this latest outrage has been made, in subtle and not so subtle ways. One contemptible example of this could be seen on a recent episode of "The A-Team." This depicted the team breaking Murdoch out of a mental hospital (a crime), while the camera panned in on Mr. T, who was sitting in the escape van wearing (you guessed it) his seat belt.

And then there was *Easy Prey*, a TV movie starring "Simon & Simon's" Gerald McRaney as serial killer Christopher Wilder. This one was a real gem. In between each brutal stabbing or shooting, on his way from killing to killing, he made sure that he was wearing his seat belt whenever he was driving. I guess this is supposed to show that even crazed maniacs on murder sprees wear their seat belts, so they can't be all bad. Now, Wilder went on his spree several years before seat belt laws were introduced, so it is easy to see that this is just another cheap and tasteless attempt to influence the public to accept mandatory seat-belt laws.

Mandatory is an ugly word, and should deserve no place in a free society unless it applies to politicians being required to operate within the framework of our Constitution without violating it. And then there are other forms of propaganda, cooked up by pressure groups and pressure group activists, all trying to mold American culture in their image.

The age old question has always been: Does art imitate life, or does life imitate art?

Well, it would appear that art is used to deceive and manipulate life in a lot of ways, at least on television, where lifestyles and character traits are promoted via TV programs and commercials. For example, a recent General Foods International Coffees commercial, with heavy feminist undertones, goes something like this: A young couple comes home from an office party, and immediately the pathetic jerk of a husband runs into the kitchen to fix his baby a cup of Swiss mocha, because she had a hard day at the office, while he probably stayed at home and did the dishes and vacuumed the floors. She says, "Oh, how did you know this was what I wanted?" And he replied, "I guess it's just man's [instead of woman's] intuition."

Obviously this is something that would sicken the Duke or any self-respectin' male, but it is a clear illustration of how even the most crass and shallow commercials can be used to try and influence people's lifestyles.

Nowadays, most television programs are lacking in originality, spirit, and depth, and are basically used as media for conveying "social" messages and themes of the most banal variety. One of the most atrocious examples of this was "M*A*S*H," which started out as a genuinely funny show, but ended up taking itself too seriously, and gradually became a soap operaish, tearjerker type of program where all the characters started developing personal problems and became deeply introspective at least once during each episode.

The basic gullibility of the American public can be seen by the fact that the last episode of M*A*S*H, broadcast on February 23, 1983, was one of the most-watched shows ever in the history of television.

Arthur Hailey's book *Hotel* was a fine, well-written piece of literature, but the TV show is just a landlubbers version of *The Love Boat*, that horrendous, dime-store romance novel come to life and translated into film.

And what would we do without all the cop shows that constantly glorify the police, the courts and the law, always trying to convince us that the police are our "pals" and not the henchmen of the thugs in power? They can be amusing to watch, and many people swallow it up voraciously until they find themselves being victimized by an overzealous "peace officer" or some unrealistic or unconstitutional law.

On one hand, you have the government pushing "nationalism" and totalitarian practices in an attempt to subjugate the public collectively, sort of like harnessing a team of horses under one whip to restrain individuality.

On the other hand, you have a wide variety of meddlers and busybodies trying to push all kinds of repressive, intolerant, and idiotic ideas and programs on the rest of the public. The American public is too gullible and trusting for their own good.

I don't know any of the political bigwigs in this country, and neither does most of the population. Why trust any of these people? Just because they hold public office? Just because they are supposedly "experts"? That's not good enough. How many people would trust a stranger in the street? Why trust one who holds public office? Because he is neatly groomed, waves a flag, and eats apple pie? Come off it already.

Obviously, just because someone looks respectable doesn't mean that he is. Adolf Hitler looked like a shoe salesman, and twenty million deaths can be laid on his doorstep.

To allow government and corporate officials to dictate morality and employ totalitarian measures is the same as allowing a couple of thugs to break into your home and start ordering you around and tell you what you can or cannot do by force.

If you think about the way the media campaigns supporting the "war on drugs," seat belt laws, military intervention in Nicaragua, and a host of other absurdities have been conducted, it is easy to see that many Hitlerian propaganda techniques and theories are employed quite regularly every day.

With this in mind, if one turns the wheel of the mental kaleidoscope of one's brain, and takes a look at reality from a fresh point of view, it could be easily apparent that every day we are witnessing the relentless, behind-the-scenes manipulation of hundreds of millions of American by the government, private interest groups, corporations, and other aggressors for their own ends. The only defense against succumbing to propaganda is to regard with suspicion and circumspection whatever news is doled out by the media, and compare it with whatever true facts, knowledge, and real information that is already on hand.

The intrinsic greatness of the U.S.A. lies in the philosophy of each and every individual possessing the freedom of choice and the right to decide for himself whether or not something is right or wrong and whether or not to do it.

Obviously, if a person considers himself an adult, then he must assume that he is capable of making decisions on all matters, whatever their nature.

To allow the government, the president, or anyone else to dictate morality or interfere in our personal lives is to bring into activization the *Fuehrerprinzip* (leader principle), in which a so-called leader decides on morality and laws for all. And where does this type of thinking and these kinds of practices lead to?

Remember the ominous words of Herman Goering, Field Marshal of the Third Reich: "I have no conscience; Adolf Hitler is my conscience."[13]

NOTES

1. Ovid Demaris, *America the Violent* (Baltimore: Penguin Books, Inc., 1970), x.
2. Ibid., 6–7.
3. Ibid., 10–11.
4. Walter C. Langer, *The Mind of Adolf Hitler* (New York: New American Library, Inc., Meridian Books, 1985), 74.
5. Ibid., 76.
6. Wayne Beissert, "Drug Test Halted As Degrading," *USA Today* (November 13, 1986), 1A.
7. Robert J. Ringer, *Looking Out for Number One* (New York: Fawcett Crest Books, 1978), 77–78.
8. C. G. Jung, *The Undiscovered Self* (New York: New American Library, Inc., Mentor Books, 1958), 26–27.
9. Friedrich Nietzsche, *Thus Spoke Zarathustra* (New York: Penguin Books, 1980), 118–119.
10. "At War With Drugs," Elaine Warren, *TV Guide* (November 29–December 5, 1986), 25.
11. Alan Bullock, *Hitler—A Study in Tyranny* (New York: Perennial Library, Harper & Row Publishers, 1971), 207.
12. Floyd G. Cullop, *The Constitution of the United States: An Introduction*, 84.
13. Walter C. Langer, *The Mind of Adolf Hitler*, 76.

Chapter Three

Corporate Culture—Adventures in Modern Serfdom

With the advent of the Industrial Revolution in the 1800s and the rapid growth of technology, America has become a country dominated by huge corporations, many of whose yearly gross profits are higher than the yearly gross national products of most of the countries in the world.

Conducting business of all types has become an everyday, all-consuming passion, and this has led to a phenomenon known as corporate culture, where position is worshipped and sacrificed to, and "values" are superficial and phony.

Major stockholders of corporations and the owners of individual businesses have become the feudal barons of today, and the employees of these corporations and companies have become modern-day serfs. The employee (the serf) relies on the employer (the land baron) for the opportunity to earn his living and his daily bread. The employer (the land baron) relies on the employee (the serf) to maintain his estate and produce the harvest (company profits). This symbiotic relationship between serf and baron is all well and good; it reflects the balance and laws of nature.

The problem begins when the baron tells the serf, "It's okay for you to work for me for eight, ten, twelve, or fourteen hours a day and make me rich, but you can't do what you want on your own time and make your own decisions and choices because I'll penalize you for it." When the serf is expected to live strictly for the baron and the baron's harvest, and is blackmailed (through urine testing programs, et cetera) into restricting his behavior and choices, then we are looking at a situation that is

CORPORATE PUPPET-SLAVE

unnatural, immoral, and unacceptable. Let's face it, in spite of the glorification of industry and technology, what universal importance is there in manufacturing automobiles to drive around in (one of the nation's and the planet's biggest industries)? Most of our technology and industry is designed to produce creature comforts, and this has led to a syndrome that could be entitled "Creature Comfort Cretinism."

"Take away my rights and freedoms, but leave me my car keys and my VCR," seems to be the prevailing attitude of those afflicted with this disease which paralyzes the intellect and spirit of an individual through the introduction of too many creature comforts, turning him or her into an indifferent idiot or cretin. To those affected by this sickness, the only important knowledge is how to read the *TV Guide* and operate the microwave oven. Rights and freedoms appear to them as abstract theories instead of important realities that they dispose of in return for material rewards.

Of course, this isn't a new phenomenon, only an escalated version. Writing in 1796, in speaking of the willingness of the many to sacrifice freedom for the sake of material comforts, de Sade stated:

> When laws were first promulgated, and the weak consented to the loss of a portion of their freedom in order to preserve the remainder, the maintenance of their possessions was undoubtedly the first thing that they desired to enjoy in peace, and the prime object of the restraints they demanded.
>
> The stronger gave their consent to laws which they were sure they could escape: the laws were made. It was decreed that every man would possess his inheritance in peace and that anyone who interfered in his possession of that inheritance would suffer punishment. But there was nothing of nature in this, nothing that she ordained, nothing that she inspired.
>
> It was all the work of men, who henceforth were divided into two classes: the first class gave up a quarter in

order to obtain the tranquil enjoyment of the rest; the second, profiting by this quarter, and realising that it could have the other three quarters whenever it liked, agreed to prevent, not the weak from being ravaged by the strong, but the weak from ravaging one another, in order that it alone could strip them at its own convenience[1]

Where does this insatiable desire for creature comforts come from, and how is it perpetuated by the "strong"?

Well, a good explanation was given by Professor Norman O. Brown when he wrote:

What the elegant laws of supply and demand really describe is the antics of an animal which has confused excrement with aliment and does not know it, and which, like infantile sexuality, pursues no "real aim."

Having no real aim, acquisitiveness, as Aristotle correctly said, has no limit. Hence the psychological premise of a market economy is not, as in classical theory of exchange, that the agents know what they want, but that they do not know what they want.

In advanced capitalist countries advertising exists to create irrational demands and keep the consumer confused; without the consumer confusion perpetuated by advertising, the economy would collapse. Thus, as Ruskin again saw, the science of political economy must perpetuate darkness and nescience (ignorance): So far, therefore, as the science of exchange relates to the advantage of one of the exchanging persons only, it is founded on the ignorance or incapacity of the opposite person. . . . It is therefore a science founded on nescience. . . . This science, alone of sciences, must, by all available means, promulgate and prolong its opposite nescience. . . . It is therefore peculiarly and alone the science of darkness."[2]

This can be seen by the way advertising is continually used to convince the public that they have some "hole" in their lives that needs "filling," that by drinking this coffee or buying that car they will achieve instant sophistication and happiness. Of course, anyone with any sense would see through such foolish premises, but a lot of sensible people seem to be steadily licking it up.

How often does someone really need a new car, or since when does drinking a particular brand of coffee make someone sophisticated? Obviously this is all part of the continuous flood of advertising mythology that is spewed out everywhere, designed to keep the wheels of industry turning.

Admittedly, we would not have the high standard of living we do today if not for industry and technology. But what good are the latest material comforts and gadgets if you have been stripped of your rights and freedoms? Or, to draw a biblical parallel, "What shall it profit a man if he gaineth the whole world, but loseth his soul?" (Mark 8:36).

Individual rights and freedom of choice seem to be taking a back seat in the corporate world in favor of company profits and conformity. Today, major corporations try to pass themselves off as modern-day gods who will provide for our every need. What next? Will priests and priestesses be installed as administrators of corporate churches, with company logos and dollar signs taking the place of the cross as items of worship?

Now let's face it; if the businessman wants to make money, that's real fine and dandy. Everybody needs a source of income or a job, and in a good sense, many businessmen are the Atlases that support the rest of the population by supplying job opportunities, services, and products. But what has to be remembered is that they are the ones getting rich, and they are very dependent upon their employees to perform their duties and functions.

When they start slapping their employees around, stripping them of their dignity, treating them like slaves, and imposing their values and will on them, then it's time they were reminded in no uncertain terms that they are getting too big for their britches, and they have to back off.

More and more, big businesses attempt to treat their employees like mischievous children who need constant supervision and correction. An example of this can be seen by the way Capital Cities-ABC, Inc., a New York-based media company, initiated the unconstitutional practice of using drug-sniffing dogs in the offices of the TV and newspaper companies under its ownership.

This is also an example of how corporations have conspired with the government with the "war on drugs." ABC-TV has heavily promoted a lot of antidrug propaganda over the past year.

Another seeming co-conspirator in this affair could be General Electric, which recently purchased NBC, and announced on September 4, 1986 that they were launching mandatory urine testing on their employees.

With large corporations in control of much of the media, is it any wonder that the totalitarian practices being promoted by the media are seen actively being perpetrated in the workplace? This is an affront to the upright dignity and self-respect of every American citizen; it seems like a throwback to yesteryear, when laborers had no protection and were victimized by the early industrial barons.

Another threat to individuality and freedom of choice is the concept of the corporation or organization man, whose role in life is comparable to a cog in a wheel. People are trained to believe that the ideal goal in life is to have a career with the company, that just being part of the "team" will give one a feeling of satisfaction. The problem is that many corporations try to turn their employees into puppets by a variety of techniques. Dress codes are one way. Regulations governing hair, mustaches, and beards are another—and then there are drug-testing programs, just to add that special touch of degradation. The corporate dictators use these methods to reinforce submissive behavior in their employees, all designed to stifle individual self-expression and freedom of choice.

What we are seeing here is the attempt, not just in the corporate world but also on a national scale, to subsume opposing ideologies, countercultures, and viewpoints through dictatorial and unconstitutional abuses of power, to create a "unified America" where each citizen is ready to blindly obey governmental policy and march out every day to make more profits for the corporate "land barons." Employers only deserve an hour's labor for an hour's pay, not full-time subservience.

My brother was recently harassed at a school he was attending in Alabama, and he wrote the following article for his school newspaper, the content of which I felt could also apply to the workplace:

> The 1985–1986 Montgomery Academy handbook states that (for gentlemen) "Hair must be neat, well-groomed, and of a reasonable length. Mustaches are not permissible." The revised edition will obviously be another attack on personal freedom of a magnitude equal or greater than its oppressive predecessor. William Pitt, the great English statesman, in his speech to Parliament on the Indian Bill (of 1783) irrevocably declared that "Necessity is the plea of every infringement of human freedom. It is the argument of tyrants; it is the creed of slaves." Infringement of human freedom has as much to do with muzzling the press as it does with stifling the individuality of our society. After all, enforcing an archaic standard of "Hair length" or a policy of "no facial hair" results only from the narrow-mindedness of individuals that are unable to understand the structure of our modern society.
>
> John Locke, the English philosopher of the Enlightenment, and whose principles flow through the Declaration of Independence, stated in his "Essay Concerning Human Understanding" that "New opinions are always suspected, and usually opposed, without any other reason than they are not already common."
>
> It is unfortunate that the rights of the individual mean so little to the people that have fought for their country, the people that have worked for their country, and the people that supported their country, because they have bypassed their freedoms to conform to an unnecessary social order that has been created by a few "privileged" tyrants (Pitt).

For as the old adage states "the laws are made for the people, not the people for the laws." It is in all ways logical that these insidious articles be revised for the welfare of the students. For if this will be tolerated now, no matter the magnitude of the offense, what greater restriction on our personal freedom will we allow?

Pablo Picasso was once quoted as saying "Anything new, anything worth doing, can't be recognized. People just don't have that much vision."

Perhaps it is time we recognize things worth doing. The most outstanding individuals in the pages of history are those who have stood outside the mainstream and have refused to be relegated to the role of team lackey. As a Salada Tea Bag tag states: "Those who follow crowds will never be followed by them."

Unfortunately, because of social repressiveness, censorship, and constant emphasis on tradition and conformity, there is a serious lack of leadership in the field of individuality.

Now, if an employee does his or her job to the best of his or her ability and regularly shows up for work, then what business is it of anyone else's if someone has long hair, wears strange clothes, has a beard or mustache, uses alcohol or drugs on their own time, or anything else? Obviously, the "privleged tyrants" (i.e., corporate executives, government officials, et cetera) want to breed legions of puppet-slaves, all neatly groomed and dressed, alcohol and drug "free," ready to be instantly obedient to their "masters." This seems to have gone unnoticed by the vast majority of the public, however. People have been trained to believe that serving the company and playing along with whatever governmental policies are in effect is the "American" way and the proper thing to do. But since every American citizen is a unique individual, the "American" way is whatever each person chooses it to be, regardless of what somebody else says. The American way is supposed to be the way of the free individual, not the corporate slave or the puppet of the Machiavellian opportunists in government office.

To be free of this yoke of oppression, individuals must be willing to dispense with tradition and established customs and practices and firmly commit themselves to the development of their own individuality and potential. People who think for themselves in every way and do as they please are almost impossible to govern and have no desire to be governed.

Of course, this is anathema to the barbarians and thugs in power, who want to control everything and everybody.

Always beware of people who call rights and liberties "privileges," for they are already under the ether and are part of the problem. They try to imply that what you have already been naturally endowed with is theirs to give or take at will, and this is not right. Maybe what we need is a National Serf Protective Association to protect employees everywhere (whether white or blue collar) from dress codes, hair-style regulations, drug-testing programs, or the rest of the authoritarian trash that a self-righteous, pompous mentality can dream up.

Freedom is sweet, and authoritarianism is ugly, and life is too short to allow oneself to be bossed around and victimized by someone else. Corporations, as we know them, are a relatively new phenomenon in human history.

The individual was here a long time before the corporation. Of course, the whole record of human rights and their violations throughout history is appalling and reads like a tragic horror story.

You would think that with progressive achievements in knowledge and learning mankind would try and make a positive change toward itself, and throw aside all these restraints and all this repression. Unfortunately, it seems that Corporate Culture, Creature Comfort Cretinism, Meddlemania, and just plain old greed and stupidity have dulled the senses and clouded the eyes of the majority of the public, and now we stand on the verge of a cultural apocalypse where individual rights and freedom of choice and self-expression will be almost nonexistent in the very near future unless every citizen in this country makes a firm commitment to say no to all the meddling and these Gestapo-type practices.

Corporate officers and executives (as well as many politicians) seem to think of themselves as contemporary aristocracy-modern royalty if you will. There seems to be no end to their high-handed, self-righteous behavior.

Underneath all the noble talk and pretentious sermonizing that these people are always oozing and dispensing, let's take a look at the way it really is.

Most big companies demand that prospective employees take a physical examination before they are hired, and in many cases, annual checkups are required.

Before cows, pigs, or sheep are sold or slaughtered, they are given careful examinations to make sure they are healthy and not diseased, and are usually checked out periodically. Horse and dog urine is tested out at racetracks, to make sure the animals aren't "doped up." Nowadays, the Meddlemaniacs in the corporate world want to check out human urine to make sure their "animals" aren't "doped up." Pretty degrading to be checked out and tested like a lowly beast of the field, wouldn't you say? Yet they always profess to have such good reasons.

Schoolchildren are told how to dress and how to cut their hair by their parents, and are usually patronized in a sanctimonious way. How many mature adults enjoy being treated like schoolchildren, or like being thought of as animals that need to be periodically checked out for "disease?"

The United States of America is a free country, where each individual is guaranteed his or her rights of liberties under the United States Constitution and the Bill of Rights.

We are all sovereign citizens, and no one, not the government, the corporate dictators, or anyone else, has any right whatsoever to infringe on us. (The Fourteenth Amendment, among others, is supposed to guarantee this.) Unfortunately, the government and the industrialists have violated the Constitution so many times and gotten away with it that it has almost become a worthless piece of paper you could use in the bathroom.

If a person is expected to live by company policies both on- and off-duty, then how can they think of themselves as members of a free society, with liberty and justice for all? Obviously, some very serious basic priorities have gotten distorted and it seems that the cause of the individual and freedom of choice has reached a crisis stage. Every time someone allows himself to give in to freedom restricting practices, it scores more points for the Constitution-busting criminals who want to rule other men.

Will the desire for creature comforts continue to rise at the expense of our rights and freedoms, or will the American public realize that liberty has a higher value than material things and make up their minds not to be stepped on and made a mockery of? Many Americans seem to have become overly spoiled, sentimental, and self-indulgent because of our vast material and financial wealth, and through the hypnotic TV eye, the liars who profess to speak truth have persuaded many to be willing to give up their rights and freedoms, in many cases, without knowing it.

In his brilliant book *Future Shock*, Alvin Toffler wrote:

> Today in the techno-societies there is an almost ironclad consensus about the future of freedom. Maximum individual choice is regarded as the democratic ideal. Yet most writers predict that we shall move further and further from this ideal.
>
> They conjure up a dark vision of the future, in which people appear as mindless consumer-creatures, surrounded by standardized goods, educated in standardized schools, fed a diet of standardized mass culture, and forced to adopt standardized styles of life.[3]

It sort of looks like we have arrived at the door of this situation which the meddlers have consciously or unconsciously helped to hasten. It is imperative that the citizens of this country re-acquaint themselves with the meaning of the words *freedom* and *liberty*, as well as the Constitution before we end up in totalitarian circumstances that are irreversible without resorting to another Civil War or American Revolution.

NOTES

1. *The Selected Writings of de Sade*, translated by Leonard de Saint-Yves (New York: Castle Books, 1954), 76–77.
2. Norman O. Brown, *Life Against Death* (Middletown, Ct.: Wesleyan University Press, 1959), 258.
3. Alvin Toffler, *Future Shock* (New York: Bantam Books, Inc., 1971), 263.

Chapter Four
Religion in America—The Simooms of Swindlers

Prudishness and smug pomposity seem to have been underlying American characteristics since the start of this country up to the present, and these two tendencies have never been more obvious than in the field of organized "religion."

It would seem that most preachers in this country have always had an inclination toward intolerance and narrow-mindedness, and because of the rapid development of the media in the last fifty years, we now have a unique phenomenon—the televangelist.

Now, admittedly, some of these people are sincere preachers of the Gospel who preach the Word earnestly and stick to strictly religious matters.

However, with a lot of these people, what you basically hear is a strange brew of political rhetoric, "religion," and right-wing dreck. In between quoting Scripture, they attack liberals and democrats (whom they accuse of being communists) and, in some of the more extreme cases, even Santa Claus and the Easter Bunny become sinister pawns of the powers of darkness, whom they sternly denounce as "enemies of Christendom."

To listen to some of them babble on behind the pulpit, you get the idea that they see themselves descending from Mount Sinai with a stone tablet grapsed in each hand.

Now, in looking back through history, one can see how closely "religions" have worked together with governments to control the masses and keep individuals in check. It should seem suspicious to any thinking individual that politicians and "religious" leaders are so chummy these days, at a time when so much repressive social phenomenon is occurring. Of course, this is nothing new.

As de Sade pointed out 191 years ago:

> Let no one doubt that religions are the cradle of despotism. The first of all the tyrants was a priest. Numa and Augustus, the first king and the first emperor of Rome, were themselves associated with the priesthood; Constantine and Clovis were abbots rather than sovereigns; Heliogabulus was the priest of the sun.
>
> In every age there was such a close link between despotism and religion that it is all too obvious that by destroying one you must undermine the other, for the very important reason that the first will always serve as law to the second.[1]

In the last few years, several of these televangelists have reached the point where they are yanking in 50 to 150 million dollars per year from public contributions, and money they pull in from hawking "religious" wares of all kinds, from tie clasps and cuff links to cassette tapes and records.

It would probably come as no surprise to find out that many of these televangelists and "religious" leaders are probably some of the prime culprits in this conspiracy to police America. A couple of them openly admit to having conferred with the president on the state of this country and so-called religious matters. Now, did Christ confer with Caesar about Roman policy or religious matters?

With such vast sums of cash at their disposal, it would be child's play to exert strong influences on political decisions and passages of "laws."

It is well known that some of these people are involved in politics and lobbying, and in their twisted quest for a return to "old-fashioned" values, they would probably stop at nothing to achieve their goals. These people have amassed powerful financial and political bases with which to perpetuate their ideas and beliefs, on a scale that is hard for the average person to understand because of the magnitude of their ramifications.

One example of how we all, as a nation, are being affected by their financial power and self-righteous attitudes is the way members of the so-called Moral Majority, which is headed by the Rev. Jerry Falwell, successfully picketed and blackmailed (by boycotting their products) the Southland Corporation into removing all adult magazines from their 7-11 grocery stores. Anyone who has ever listened to Falwell sermonize on his Sunday morning TV show has heard how opposed he is to the pornographers and smut merchants that he feels are poisoning the land.

Now how much does it take to figure that this was a deliberate attempt to dictate and enforce morality through economic sanctions? You have to ask yourself what this guy really stands for when he passes himself off as a "lover of freedom," but at the same time interferes actively with the freedom of choice of others.

Liberty is defined by Webster's *Dictionary* as meaning "freedom from bondage, captivity, restraint, et cetera."

Reverend Falwell has named his university Liberty Bible College, but in light of the 7-11/Southland episode, such a title sounds preposterous. The removal from 7-11 stores of adult magazines is a reality, not a piece of fiction.

And several months after all this happened, out comes "The Meese Commission Report on Pornography," a contrived, twelve-hundred-page piece of pure pseudomoral propaganda, which, according to the ACLU's Barry Lynn is "full of factual errors, preposterous legal theories, undocumented allegations and unwarranted hysterics about the effect of sexually explicit material on viewers and readers."[2] How could these two occurrences be unrelated?

Now think about this. One hundred years ago, these sideshow hustlers would have been peddling bottles of snake oil or some kind of bogus, cure-all medicine out of the back of a covered wagon, staying just one step ahead of the sheriff. Now they have updated their methodology, using the media to appeal to the emotional and spiritual appetites of the masses, while they force their beliefs and values on millions of people and rake in as much dough as possible. Keep those checks and money orders coming in, folks! We take Visa and Master Charge, too!

How long will the public allow themselves to be fleeced by these money changers in their television temples?

After each bellicose spewing of ridiculous and intolerant nonsense they always make a pitch for cash contributions ("love offerings"), as they can go on and on with their self-righteous little crusades. And every day, millions of red, white, and blue suckers continue to support them.

How does this work? By passing themselves off as oracles of divine wisdom and vessels of virtue, they persuade legions of individuals to doubt the validity of their own consciousness and intellect, and to look up to Mr. TV Preacher as their spiritual commander-in-chief, always ready to hear the words of wisdom from on high.

If someone wants to get closer to God or be saved, what do they need besides a Bible and a place to pray?

Who needs Reverend Loudmouth's "10 Steps to Salvation" tape cassette series, for a mere $49.95?

Of course, this type of spiritual and intellectual intimidation was around a long time before television existed, which is evidenced by another quotation of de Sade, who must have noticed the same techniques being practiced when he wrote:

> Every principle is a judgment, every judgment is the consequence of experience, and experience is acquired only by the exercise of the sense.
>
> It follows from this, obviously that religious principles are related to nothing and are not in any way inborn. How could reasonable beings, you will continue, ever have been persuaded that the most difficult thing for them to comprehend was the most essential to them. Because they have been greatly frightened, and when man is afraid, he ceases to reason.
>
> Above all, because they have been advised to suspect

their reason, and conflict in the mind gives rise to faith in anything and analysis of nothing. Tell them that ignorance and fear are the twin foundations of all religions.

The uncertainty in which man finds himself over his relationship with his God is precisely the motive which attaches him to his religion. Man is afraid in the darkness, physically as much as morally; fear becomes habitual in him and develops into need. If he had nothing more to hope for or fear, he would believe that something was lacking.[3]

At the time de Sade was writing, the Catholic Church was the predominant "religious" power, and this organization has to rank as one of the longest lasting and most profitable "religious" corporations that has ever existed.

How could any sane or reasonable person think that a guy in a fancy costume (the head of the corporation) could be God on earth? According to Ralph Woodrow, in his book *Babylon Mystery Religion*, the basis for this belief is that the Pope, "—according to Catholic doctrine—is the earthly head of the church and successor of the apostle Peter."[4]

Mr. Woodrow goes on to say:

> Beginning with Peter, the Catholic Church claims a succession of popes which has continued to this day. This is a very important part of Roman Catholic doctrine. But do the scriptures teach that Christ ordained ONE man to be above all others in his church? Can we find any scriptural authority for the office of a pope, a supreme pontiff? Did the early Christians recognize Peter as such?
>
> To the contrary, the scriptures clearly show there was to be an equality among the members of the church and that "CHRIST is the head of the church" (Eph. 5:23) not the pope![5]

What this doctrine basically tries to promote is the myth that each and every pope was a man of cleanliness and godliness on the level of Christ Himself, or at the very least, His servant Peter. However, the record is there to prove this wrong.

According to Mr. Woodrow, many of whose references come out of the *Catholic Encyclopedia*, some of the popes were the most vicious and depraved criminals that ever lived.

For instance, Innocent III (1198–1216), who was estimated to have had over one million people killed in the Inquisition. Boniface VIII (1294–1303), of whom was said: "Scarcely any possible crime was omitted—infedelity, heresy, simony, gross and unnatural immorality, idolatry, magic, loss of the Holy Land, death of Celestine V, etc."[7]

And here's a real special one: Alexander VI (1492–1503), whose real name was Rodergio Borgia (father of Lucretia, the infamous poisoner), who lived in public incest with his two sisters and daughter and who, "on October 31, 1501, conducted a sex orgy in the Vatican, the equal of which for sheer horror has never been duplicated in the annals of human history."[8] October 31 (Halloween, or All Saints Eve) is one of three major "holy days" on the calendars of devil worshippers, which adds a sinister undertone to this particular pope.

This is not to say that all popes were or are criminals and frauds. It is simply to point out that the reality is much different than what the papacy would like the world to believe.

In a discussion of the Protestant reformer Martin Luther and his views on the Catholic church, Normal O. Brown wrote:

> Ultimately, Luther's conviction that the Papacy is a demonry rests on his rejection of outwardly good works—that is to say, his conviction that visible reality is under the domination of the Devil. In Luther's eyes the ultimate sin of the Papacy is its accommodation to this world, its attempts to spiritualize this world: in psychoanalytical terms, its allegiance to the Platonic-Aristotelian ideal of sublimation.
>
> Given Luther's sense of the irredeemable (until the Second Coming) evil of this world, the effort to spiritualize this world only confused the two realms which according

to Lutheran theology must be kept separate, the flesh and the spirit.

The Papacy has so confused worldly and spiritual rule, that neither has stayed in its own power and right.

Under the Papacy the great and special secret has been forgotten, that Christ's kingdom is not a temporal, perishable, earthly kingdom, but a spiritual one.

But this confusion of good works with grace, of the earthly and the heavenly, is, as we have seen, the finest trick of the Devil, the Father of Lies, in order to secure man's allegiance to the world and the flesh and the Devil.

Hence, the Papacy exhibits all the characteristics of demonic possession. First of all the Papacy exhibits a drive for power: "That which Christ denied and avoided, namely worldly rule, power and glory, that the Papacy pursues with raging madness." The structure of this power drive is essentially demonic, like the Devil himself, and like capitalism, the Pope seeks to the prince of this world and God on earth.[9]

These last few pages were not meant as a condemnation of any individual belonging to the Catholic religion, but a condemnation of what is probably a corrupt, man-made system promulgated by greedy men for their own glory and enrichment, who have aided and abetted dictators, political and otherwise, down through the centuries, in deceiving and controlling nations and individuals. And this is just one specific "religious" institution.

There are a lot more copycats and imitators, as well as incidental psychopaths (e.g., the Reverend Jim Jones, who murdered nine hundred of his followers in the Guyana tragedy).

As with the mass media, religions and religious organizations have become tools of authoritarian control that deliberately manipulate and suppress millions of American citizens every day. If they can't control you with the sword of the law, then they try to bind you spiritually with "religion."

The government outrightly advocates and promotes "religion in America" via television spots sponsored by an agency called the Ad Council. No doubt this is to promote the Marxian maxim that "religion is the opiate of the masses." The idea here is to keep your eyes and mind occupied with a lot of pie-in-the-sky nonsense, while they are pulling a lot of underhanded business right under your nose.

An example of how some of these people attempt to undermine the minds of viewers can be seen in a quotation from the July 7, 1986, broadcast of a Jimmy Swaggart TV show, in which he called the science of psychology "modern witchcraft, with occult roots."

Obviously, the idea here is to persuade people who need counseling for mental problems to distrust psychiatrists and psychologists (who are trained to deal with such matters), and instead turn to Jimmy Swaggert for the answers, while they are making out a check or money order to send to him. Most of these people specialize in working on people's emotions, those Achilles' heels that usually border on the irrational.

Rarely are any constructive, fact-based, intellectual ideas introduced or any calm, cerebral discussions carried on. Most of the time, it's the same repetitious rabble-rousing and emotional carrying-on that seems to have an almost narcotic effect on most of the audience. Once a day, or once a week, millions of Americans tune in to get their "fix."

Many of these preachers seem to be afflicted with mediocre mentalities, in spite of their money-making abilities. Whenever they are faced with abstract or visionary ideas and philosophies, they fall back upon and embrace "old-fashioned" values.

This is a clear-cut example of mental midgetry, the sign of an unimaginative, intellectually stagnant mentality that is inevitably forced to hide behind obscure and outdated points of view because they possess no original ideas or understanding of their own. The swaggering Swaggart is one of the top grossers in the televangelist field, regularly yanking in between 140 and 150 million dollars a year. He also, according to journalist Michelle Mayron in an article she wrote in the December 1986 issue of *Spin* Magazine, is something of a dictator within the realm of the Swaggart ministries, where Ministries employees are expected to submit to mandatory lie-detector tests and mandatory weight-loss programs when they appear to be gaining a few pounds. According to the same article, Swaggart lives in a multimillion dollar mansion, with several swimming pools, three Lincolns, and a Mercedes.[10]

Not bad, eh?

I witnessed a Swaggart display earlier this year, after he had worked himself up into a frenzy on one of his TV broadcasts. He was all wrapped up in some intolerant subject, and he was saying, "If you don't like this country, fella, then why don't you get on out!" Did you ever notice that the people who are always saying, "America—love it or leave it," are usually a rigid, narrow-minded bunch that are ignorant of the Constitution and its implications, and don't seem to understand what individual liberty and freedom of choice is all about?

If they don't like living in a country where freedom and liberty are supposed to reign supreme, then they should take their own advice and move to an Iron or Bamboo Curtain country, where just about everything is restricted and governed by totalitarian authority. A recent example of a charlatan being uncovered was shown on a segment of the CBS newmagazine "West 57th."

A magician known as the Amazing Randy, who has been trying to expose phony faith healers and their ilk, and has written a book on the subject, exposed televangelist Peter Popoff and his use of electronic gimmickry. Apparently, Popoff had been running a faith-healing scam, and part of this scam involved his approaching members of the audience and telling them their names and their problems, supposedly by the aid of the Holy Spirit.

However, with the aid of an electronic monitoring device, the Amazing Randy discovered that these people had been interviewed earlier by members of Popoff's staff and their names and problems were relayed to Popoff onstage via a small radio transmitter/receiver system by his wife and staff members.

Ominously enough, within a week of this exposé, Popoff's programs were no longer listed in *TV Guide* or broadcast on the air. Probably the rest of the hucksters got together and told him,

"Look, the jig is up, you're going to ruin it for all of us if you don't take a hike."

Now, before the electronic age, can you imagine how many of these frauds managed to deceive and bilk millions of people without getting caught?

A statement on a Norman Rockwell painting that depicts a variety of people praying says: "Each according to his own conscience." This insightful portrait illustrates a truth that should hold true not only with prayer or religious beliefs, but with any other practice or activity in a free society.

A society cannot be considered free where morality (which concerns the innermost parts of a person's soul) and freedom of choice are restricted, defined, and enforced by a self-appointed group of Meddlemaniacs and Snoopy Sniffers who have come to the erroneous conclusion that they are morally superior to others.

These "moral" crusaders and "religious" leaders who are trying to prescribe and dictate morality, and censor other people, are really only interested in policing the personal lives of others, using their shallow "Sunday School" type of values as a yardstick and a billy club.

Think about the previously quoted excerpts from *America the Violent* in chapter two dealing with the Pilgrims (who considered themselves "saints" and were insufferably self-righteous and hurt many innocent people with their witch-hunts), and then watch these guys bellowing away on their Sunday morning TV shows and think about the repressive and intolerant cultural and social phenomena occurring at the present time, and then ask yourself if it isn't entirely possible that we are still suffering from the self-righteous attitudes and intolerant prejudices of modern-day Pilgrim-type meddlers working in cahoots with the government to suppress and control the public. We should all remember what happened to innocent people because of "religious" organizations like the Inquisition.

The more serious and determined meddlers are actively persecuting those who disagree with them, and in their frenzied, self-righteous fury, have a hard time realizing that they are stepping on the freedoms and Constitutional rights of others, and are violating the sanctity of their personal lives.

Religious beliefs are a personal and private matter, and are the private concern of each individual.

Who needs these sanctimonious loudmouths on TV spewing their preposterous and antiquated ideas out on the public?

Suppose, just for the sake of pure speculation, that the world is run by one hundred or two hundred individuals who own all the land and wealth of the world, and for whom governments and religions are their puppet shows and court jesters, that they use to keep the masses under control. If there was any validity to such a speculation, then that would more or less make 99 percent of the people on the earth out to be a bunch of fools, wouldn't it? Even if there were no substance to such a perception, wouldn't such an idea still indicate that things shouldn't be taken at face value? Besides condemning the Catholic hierarchy for their desire for worldly power and glory, Luther also condemned their avaricious spirit.

Quoting Professor Brown once again (who quotes Luther):

> But money is the ultimate powerful word of the Devil; hence the Papacy reveals its allegiance to the Devil in its capitalistic spirit.
>
> The God of the Papists is Mammon.
>
> In Luther's denunciation of papal avarice, the affinity between the Papacy and the spirit of capitalism is seen particularly in the commercialization of ceremonies, such as the sale of indulgences. The dispute over the sale of indulgences dramatizes the anti-capitalistic spirit of the Reformation.
>
> In Luther's eyes, "The Papists have made out of God a merchant, who would give the kingdom of Heaven not freely, out of grace, but for money and human achievement."[11]

Wouldn't it seem possible that certain parallels could be drawn between the Papacy and their love for money, power, and glory, and today's televangelists who are seen coast to coast, and yank in vast amounts of greenbacks?

A great many outrages have been perpetrated in the name of Christ by self-righteous, narrow-minded nincompoops, and a great many more are still being perpetrated.

An article in the Falwell/Moral Majority propaganda sheet "Liberty (?) Report" expresses dismay over the fact that state officials in Mississippi had shut down a "concentration camp" for "troubled" teenage girls called Bethesda Home for Girls in Hattiesburg. Obviously, the state did the right thing, since not only were the female victims of this place kept under the most austere conditions, they were also viciously paddled for such "crimes" as singing rock'n'roll tunes or running away (who could blame them?).

It's hard to believe that in modern times, in the "land of the free," such archaic and cruel practices would be tolerated anywhere. This kind of stuff supposedly went out with the Dark Ages.

Kurt Seligmann gives an example of such a place that existed 328 years ago, before people supposedly "knew better":

> Antoinette Bourignon, the only survivor of her family, wishing to make pious use of the estate she had inherited, founded a school for homeless children. In 1658, with the permission of the Bishop of Lisle in Flanders, the school was transformed into a cloister. The girls were kept, as she says, under strict discipline.
> No mention is made as to whether they were asked how they felt about being placed in a cloister.
> After three years, thirty-two of the pensioners were discovered to be witches. The treatment of the girls was, in accordance with the views of the times, rather rigorous.
> Madame Bourignon, responsible for this convent of minors, reports that every Friday they had to humiliate themselves by admitting their faults in the public hall. These pious exercises were followed by corrections, by whipping, or by confinement in a place called the prison.

One girl of fifteen unlocked the prison door and returned to the class, which was considered by Madame Bourignon an act of witchcraft. The girl declared she had been delivered from her imprisonment by a black man. Three pastors were called in, and upon examining the culprit, discovered that she had a devil. Another girl who was to have been whipped declared that the "crime" she had committed was accomplished with the help of somebody and that she would confess everything if she were not beaten.

"Taking her aside in my chamber, she told me that it was the devil. He was a handsome youth, a little taller than herself."

Such children-devils must have pleased the other girls, for shortly afterwards, thirty-two novices told about their little man devils who were kind to them, caressing them day and night, escorting them to witches festivals, etc.

It seems quite clear that the girls, having experienced but little affection in Madame Bourignon's establishment, compensated their sad existence with day dreams of an adventurous life. They preferred to be exorcized to being penned in and fustigated (whipped).

Madame Bourignon reports also that she lodged adults, such as a girl of twenty-two, whose confessions were those of a disturbed adult. Having been subjected for eight months to exorcism and penance, she admitted to having regularly attended the nocturnal assemblies of the Sabbath, "where every devil brought from day to day his love, whether male or female . . . "

The exorcisms continued with admonitions, prayers, interrogations, punishments, until the devil appeared to Madame Bourignon in the form of a little wrinkled woman with a wry mouth.

It is not reported whether this wealthy spinster endured now the treatment she had found convenient for her pupils, and whether she was exorcized, admonished and punished.

The three pastors lost patience and the affair was

brought to court. The judges were extremely lenient with these "criminals." Only one, an adult, was imprisoned—she had begged to be put to death. The little tract ends gracefully, that it "was never known what since has become of her."[12]

It seems that today we have plenty of contemporary "Madame Bourignons" who willingly brutalize their charges to exorcise their "drug devils" or "alcohol demons."

The "Beat 'Em & Boss 'Em" school of "straightening out" teenagers is a throwback to the Middle Ages, and these places should be shut down for good, and their sadistic owners and directors thrown into prison.

In conclusion, it seems that it is high time to clean house and rid ourselves of freedom haters, religious oppressors, and all the co-conspirators of the governmental dictators that want to perpetuate outdated and archaic nonsense.

Draw your own conclusions; after all, I would think that anyone who reads this book would be interested in freedom of choice and thought. It is up to each individual to think for himself, discover his own potential, and seek the truth.

Some people might question my quoting the notorious Marquis de Sade throughout this book, especially on the subject of religion. But de Sade was a very learned man, and a lot of his statements are perfectly valid if you consider the following quotation by our third president, Thomas Jefferson:

> In every country and in every age, the priest has been hostile to liberty. He is always in alliance with the despot . . . they have perverted the purest religion ever preached to man into mystery and jargon, unintelligible to all mankind, and therefore the safer engine for their purpose.[13]

Consider the earlier statement of de Sade about "religion being the cradle of despotism," and consider the above quote of Mr. Jefferson. They could have been written by the same person, almost. Obviously, a lot of people have come to the same conclusion. I would like to close this chapter by quoting Dr. Carl Jung on the subject of individuality and Christianity:

> Firstly, the individual psyche, just because of its individuality, is an exception to the statistical rule and is therefore robbed of one of its main characteristics when subjected to the leveling influence of statistical evaluation. Secondly, the Churches grant it validity only in so far as it acknowledges their dogmas—in other words, when it surrenders to a collective category.
>
> In both cases the will to individuality is regarded as egotistic obstinacy. Science devalues it as subjectivism, and the Churches condemn it morally as heresy and spiritual pride.
>
> As to the latter charge, it should not be forgotten that, unlike other religions, Christianity holds at its core a symbol which has for its content the individual way of life of a man, the Son of Man, and that it even recognizes this individuation process as the incarnation and revelation of God Himself.
>
> Hence, the development of the self acquires a new significance whose full implications have hardly begun to be appreciated, because too much attention to externals blocks the way to immediate inner experience. Were not the autonomy of the individual the secret longing of many people, this hard-pressed phenomenon would scarcely be able to survive the collective suppression either morally or spiritually.[14]

NOTES

1. *The Selected Writings of de Sade*, 97.
2. Philip Nobile and Eric Nadles, "A Magna Carta For Censors," *Forum* Magazine (September 1986), 46.
3. *The Selected Writings of de Sade*, 96.

4. Ralph Woodrow, *Babylon Mystery Religion* (Ralph Woodrow Evangelistic Association, Inc., 1986), 74.
5. Ibid., 74.
6. Ibid., 94.
7. Ibid., 94.
8. Ibid., 96–97.
9. Norman O. Brown, *Life Against Death*, 228.
10. Michelle Mayron, "O Brother," *Spin* Magazine (December 1986), 60.
11. Norman O. Brown, *Life Against Death*, 228–29.
12. Kurt Seligman, *Magic, Supernaturalism and Religion* (New York: Pantheon Books, 1948), 168–69.
13. George Seldes, *The Great Thoughts*, 208.
14. C. G. Jung, *The Undiscovered Self*, 59–60.

Chapter Five
Politics and the Law

In this mousetrap called civilization, in which our privacy and freedoms are constantly in danger, we are faced with a malevolent "institution" known as "law and order."

This "institution" is the main device used by the government and other assorted meddlers to control and victimize the public. Not only are we overly burdened with too many "laws" and too much legislation, we are also today facing a group of people in power whose biggest passion seems to be enforcing "laws" by whatever means available to them (whether moral or immoral, legal or illegal), and who want to victimize and punish the population. In his book *Thus Spoke Zarathustra*, Nietzsche warned "Always mistrust those in whom the urge to punish is strong."[1]

Obviously, there is something fundamentally wrong with anyone that zealously sets out to prosecute and condemn others.

Nowadays, almost everything one says or does seems to stand in violation of some "law," because the bureaucrats have spent so much time making so many laws.

The entire legal and judicial system has become so cumbersome and bloated with all kinds of ridiculous, repressive, and absurd "laws," you have to wonder why every citizen in the country hasn't ended up being arrested for something.

In this supposedly "free" country, there are "laws" being passed every day that infringe on our rights, invade our privacy, and make life more difficult in general.

What really is law?

I think Robert J. Ringer explained it best with his definition of "natural" law:

> Every man has the natural right to pursue his own happiness in any way he chooses and to retain ownership over all the fruits of his labor, so long as he does not forcibly interfere with the same rights of others.[2]

This is a very lucid, crystal-clear explanation of law, one that should apply to a free society.

Mr. Ringer goes on to say:

> To say that laws are necessary to protect individuals sounds all right until you realize that most laws interfere with the freedom of individuals—particularly the endless number of absurd, victimless-crime laws on the books. How can any group of people—whether it calls itself a government or any other name—know what's good for you when you have desires, ambitions, needs, beliefs and standards different from anyone else's? How can they act in your best interest when they don't even know you? Only you can decide what's best for you; anyone who tries to do it for you, through force, is an aggressor and is in violation of natural law. No matter what kind of fancy words one uses to decorate the facts, the truth always remains: government restrains you, and restraint violates natural law.[3]

These are sound words of wisdom on Mr. Ringer's part, from which we could all benefit.

The "war on crime" and all this law enforcement hooey reminds me of a true story my grandfather told me about the sheriff of a small town located near the city he lived in.

Things were slow most of the time (crime-wise, that is), and this particular sheriff knew he had to prove on a regular basis that he was worth the salary he was being paid by the citizens of the town. So, once a week, usually on a weekend night, he would have several of his cronies dress up like robbers, and they would stage a phony holdup somewhere in town, and the sheriff would then chase them down the main street of the town, guns blazing, just to bamboozle the citizenry into thinking they needed a sheriff around to keep things under control.

Like unions, a lot of law enforcement agencies started out with good intentions and a good purpose. But now they have become, in many ways, the harsh, totalitarian tools of the would-be dictators who have managed to manipulate themselves into government office.

Whenever some bureaucrats or politicians decide they don't like something or they want to make life more difficult for their fellow Americans, they pass a "law" and use the police forces to make sure that it is inflicted on the public.

And the real hypocrisy lies in the fact that at the same time that these government officials are passing laws left and right, which they expect each and every citizen to obey, they themselves are breaking the laws of the land.

A recent example of this lawbreaking occurred in July and August of 1986, when U.S. military troops were shipped to Bolivia to help "clean up" the cocaine "menace."

United States Code 22, Section 2291, also known as the Mansfield Amendment, passed in 1976, clearly states:

> Notwithstanding any other provision of law, no officer or employee of the United States may engage or participate in any direct police arrest action in any foreign country with respect to narcotics control activities.
>
> No such officer or employee shall interrogate or be present at the interrogation of any United States person arrested in any foreign country with respect to narcotics control efforts.[4]

This is an outright and blatant criminal activity. No matter what self-righteous, pompous excuses they make, the fact remains the same: the United States Government broke the laws of the land.

And what about the recently exposed Iran-Contra affair? This

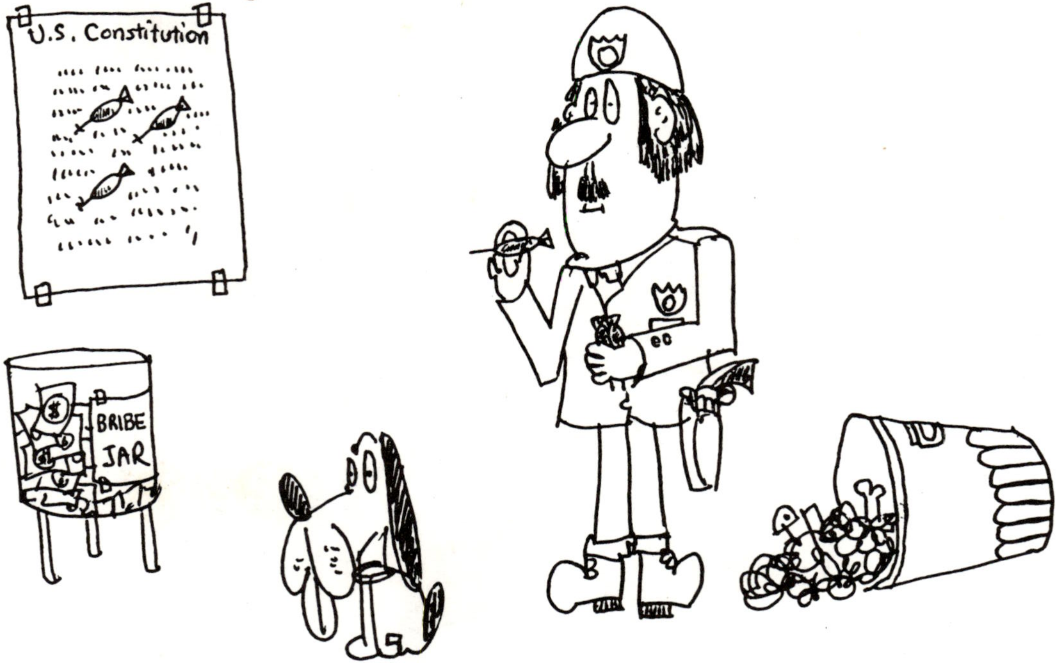
U.S. Constitution
BRIBE JAR

involved the shipping and sale of 12 million dollars' worth of military weapons to Iran, a totalitarian terrorist state that several years back held fifty-two Americans hostage for 444 days.

The profits from this venture were said to be to go to the Contra forces in Nicaragua to aid in their fight against the Sandinistas.

Now, in the summer of 1986, U.S. forces staged a military attack against Libya, killing innocent Libyan citizens in a so-called attempt to thwart terrorism. Then, just a few short months later, the U.S. government gets caught sending arms to another totalitarian state that sponsors terrorism. Just what kind of two-faced double-dealing is going on here? Of course, just about everybody in Washington, D.C. is denying any involvement in the whole affair.

The whole thing has been blamed on the renegade actions of a few lower echelon government officials acting without authorization, something that only someone with the I.Q. of a fruit fly would believe.

Even less reassuring was Ronald Reagan's Presidential Address concerning the matter. There he was—stammering, sweating, blushing—looking for all the world like a naughty schoolboy that had been caught with his hands in the cookie jar as he feebly attempted to deny any part in the swindle.

Now let's face it, when the so-called "good guys," who are always preaching law and order, actively break the laws of the land and start employing police state tactics on the sovereign citizens of this constitutional country, then that puts them in the same category with the so-called "bad guys," and you need a program to figure out who is who.

It is good to remember that the "law" is a dangerous weapon in the wrong hands, where many innocent men and women are victimized and/or imprisoned.

No doubt, many people that are in jail today were probably framed for stepping out of line or disagreeing with government policy. True freedom can only be known or perceived by living it; limitations come under the province of rules and regulations.

How can anyone know what freedom is if they have spent

their lives toeing someone else's lines or obeying someone else's rules? Obviously, they can't. And it is precisely this lack of experience and ignorance of what freedom really means that allow dictators and meddlers to manipulate the public and use doubletalk to pull the wool over the eyes of the people.

Another quotation from Dr. Jung helps illustrate this.

> One would therefore do well to possess some "imagination of evil," for only the fool can permanently neglect the conditions of his own nature.
>
> In fact this negligence is the best means of making him an instrument of evil.
>
> Harmlessness and naivete are as little helpful as it would be for a cholera patient and those in his vicinity to remain unconscious of the contagiousness of the disease.[5]

If the public were more careful in scrutinizing the government, and less trusting of the "law" and law-enforcement agents, it would be almost impossible for them to introduce totalitarian measures or violate our privacy or our rights.

Of course, with the profusion of television programs that glorify the police, the courts, and the legal system in general, most people are naturally predisposed toward blind faith in the law and the police.

And now we are faced with a situation where the current government wants to turn this country into a police state and suspend or do away with our constitutional freedoms.

It seems that the fanatical right-wing extremism being perpetrated by government officials, "religious" leaders, and certain corporate executives stems from a psychological phenomenon described by Alvin Toffler as "reversionism."

> A third common response to future shock is obsessive reversion to previously successful adaptive routines that are now irrelevant and inappropriate.
>
> The Reversionist sticks to his previously programmed decisions and habits with dogmatic desperation. The more

change threatened from without, the more meticulously he repeats past modes of action. His social outlook is regressive. Shocked by the arrival of the future, he offers hysterical support for the not-so-status quo, or he demands, in one masked form or another, a return to the glories of yesteryear.

The Barry Goldwaters and George Wallaces of the world appeal to his quivering gut through the politics of nostalgia. Police maintained order in the past; hence, to maintain order, we need only supply more police.

Authoritarian treatment of children worked in the past; hence, the troubles of the present spring from permissiveness. The middle-aged, right-wing reversionist yearns for the simple, ordered society of the small town—the slow-paced social environment in which his old routines were appropriate. Instead of adapting to the new, he continues automatically to apply the old solutions, growing more and more divorced from reality as he does so.[6]

This nationwide emphasis on enforcing repressive social phenomenon and returning to "old-fashioned" values definitely appears to be due to a large-scale outbreak of "Reversionism."

The rehashes of old TV programs and movies reflects the nostalgic desire to return to the past. One current TV show, "Crime Story," is set back in the 1960s, when cops were supposedly tougher and the law was enforced better. (Any program with a title like "Crime Story" should have as its focus the activities going on in the federal and state governments.)

Nowadays, you hear vague rumblings about "the law of the land," and how it is going to be enforced.

Would it be too fantastic to suppose that this propaganda campaign called the "war on drugs" could be a clever scheme to take over this country and place the nation under martial law?

The president and many members of Congress and the Senate want to bring in the military, and increase their involvement in this hysterical fiasco. Is it possible that they have it in mind to "take over?"

Authority should always be suspect and subject to harshest scrutiny. This is supposed to be government by the people and for the people.

All politicians and government officials should be subject to our authority as a free people at all times.

What it comes down to is this: the salaries of these government officials (from the President on down) are paid by our taxes, and this makes us (the taxpayers) their employers, and them our employees.

When they get out of line or excessively violate company policy, they should be summarily fired just like any bad employee. Instead of covering up for each other, if one official knows of wrongdoing, then he should come forth and inform the public (his employers) as to what is going on. Otherwise, he is violating the trust of his employers.

As stated before, the Constitution and the Bill of Rights were written in such a way so that every American citizen could understand what they are entitled to. However, the government and other totalitarianists have a clever device they use called "legal interpetation." By implying that judges and legal "experts" are imbued with a higher, mystical understanding of such affairs, they are able to use the "interpretation" scam to circumvent, bypass, and distort the Constitution and Bill of Rights.

No matter what these people say, though, if they are promoting something unconstitutional, then they are promoting the violation of the supreme law of the land.

What we really seem to be lacking is an objective, nonsectarian approach to leadership in this country.

What does democracy in America come down to these days? Simply that whoever can con more votes out of the people than the next guy can slip in behind the driver's seat of the national or state "car," and proceed to drive down whatever roads he likes, whether anyone else likes it or not.

Once in power, the dictator instinct seems to go right to their heads.

The last thing we need are people who use political office or legalism to force their beliefs and values on the rest of the public. Many people have heard of or remember a socio-political phenomenon in the 1950s called McCarthyism, in which a certain senator named Joseph McCarthy initiated a witch-hunt against the public to ferret out and prosecute suspected Communists, a campaign which ended up disrupting and destroying many innocent lives. Today, *McCarthyism* is a pseudonym for any kind of political witch-hunt.

Unfortunately, we are currently faced with another socio-political phenomenon which is just as threatening as McCarthyism. This syndrome could be termed "Reaganism," which is characterized by smug, self-righteous behavior, the initiation of totalitarian and unconstitutional practices, and a careless, callous disregard for the rights, privacy, and beliefs of others.

This phenomenon seems to have found fertile ground, since the basic herd instinct inherent in most individuals has driven people together into "society," which could be likened to a kindergarten classroom, with government officials playing the roles of teachers or playground monitors.

And now the "classroom rules" are becoming more rigid and intolerant, and the "teachers" are taking themselves too seriously.

A lot of this is probably due, once again, to television.

Ronald Reagan seems to be making regular Presidential Addresses; congressional sessions are regularly broadcast on the cable-TV network C-SPAN. Knowing they have a mass audience and supposed "expert" status, they seem to get carried away and start hamming it up something fierce.

Every day millions of people march to the tune the pipers have called, and if you ask them why, they just say, "I don't know, I guess I'm just a goose-steppin' fool."

Nietzsche once wrote:

> For today the petty people have become lord and master: they all preach submission and acquiescence and prudence and diligence and consideration and the long et cetera of petty virtues.[7]

Now, today, not content with simply voicing their silly, trivial beliefs and values, the Meddlemaniacs are using law and order and law-enforcement agencies to boss around the rest of the nation and make their viewpoints stick.

Basically, it seems what they want to do is turn the clock back fifty years and nurture a kind of puritanical prudishness and sanctimoniousness, while at the same time stifling the individual self-expression and free choice of people with opposing ideologies and viewpoints.

This is probably an extreme right-wing reaction to the liberalism and left-wing philosophizing of the sixties and early seventies, but that doesn't make it right or acceptable.

If these fine "moral" people and these self-righteous politicians want a place to live where everything is the way they want it, and their preposterous political philosophies can prevail, then they should buy a big piece of land somewhere and live outside the rest of the world, like the Amish people. Then they could boss each other around and police each other and interfere in each other's business and violate each other's rights. Maybe they could even rent some people to come in and be "puppets for a Day."

At any rate, they should avoid meddling and interfering with the rest of the population.

And what about the way the military is constantly glorified on television, on billboards, radio commercials and in newspaper ads? Between ads that proclaim: "Be all that you can be," and all the Selective Service registration media announcements that are regularly broadcast, it seems that there is an onrunning campaign to keep every branch of the service "beefed up."

No doubt, most of this is obvious propaganda designed to support the expenditure of billions of our tax dollars on military equipment and hardware, as well as experimental (and probably unnecessary) military programs such as "Star Wars."

However, some of this seems to be designed to stir up a spirit of militaristic nationalism in the public; and with the invasion of Grenada, the recent attacks on Libya, the proposed $100 million aid package to Nicaragua, and the shipping of U.S. troops to Bolivia, one has to wonder if the Reagan Administration isn't itching to get this country into another war.

After the tragedy and humiliation of Vietnam, you would think that they would want to leave well enough alone. And it is always the people who are willing to start wars that expect others to risk their lives fighting in them.

What we basically suffer from in this country is too much government, which not only threatens our personal privacy and rights, but which is also one of the biggest drains on our economy.

In his excellently detailed book *Fat City*, Donald Lambro lists one hundred nonessential government programs that were, at that time, sucking up $100 billion dollars a year, with the taxpayers footing the bill. Some of these included: $200,000 per year for personal chefs for Cabinet secretaries,[8] $893,000 per year for automatic elevator operators in the Capitol (the elevators, by the way, are push-button and require no operator),[9] $40,000 for the Congressional floral service,[10] $4.8 million for chauffered limousines for 175 federal officials,[11] and $2 million for the Pentagon's "top brass" dining rooms.[12]

They were also spending $114,485 per year to maintain a private gymnasium for the House of Representatives[13] and $97,801 per year to maintain a private gymnasium for members of the Senate,[14] not to mention $28,000 per year to maintain VIP lodges and retreats.[15] So, while they squander our tax dollars and pass legislation that makes our lives more difficult, these elected officials seem to have been treating themselves like royalty and indulging themselves at our expense.

Now it would definitely seem that the American public should take a closer look at the way this country is being run, and perhaps take inventory of their priorities. After all, politics is just a corrupt pseudoscience, and many things that are "illegal" shouldn't be; they have been made that way by self-righteous meddlers and Snoopy Sniffers. Otherwise, this country is liable to end up in a constitutional and cultural cul-de-sac, and the basic complexion and nature of this country will be irreparably damaged and changed.

Our Constitution and freedom of choice is what has made America the greatest nation on the planet. To allow law-and-order fanatics and politicians to infringe on our rights, privacy, and freedom of choice is to turn our backs on this country and Constitution.

Summing up "laws" and law and order in general and the folly of this barbarous institution, I think a quotation by the Roman philosopher Demonax (circa A.D. 150) best illustrates things: "Probably all laws are useless; for good men do not want laws at all, and bad men are made no better by them."[16]

NOTES

1. Friedrich Nietzsche, *Thus Spoke Zarathustra*, 24.
2. Robert J. Ringer, *Looking Out for Number One*, 24.
3. Ibid., 240.
4. Dean Latimes, "You All Sold Your Flag," *High Times* Magazine (August 1986), 20.
5. C. G. Jung, *The Undiscovered Self*, 109.
6. Alvin Toffler, *Future Shock*, 359–30.
7. Friedrich Nietzsche, *Thus Spoke Zarathustra*, 298.
8. Donald Lambro, *Fat City: How Washington Wastes Your Taxes* (Regnery-Gateway, 1980), 179.
9. Ibid., 191.
10. Ibid., 208.
11. Ibid., 223.
12. Ibid., 159.
13. Ibid., 195.
14. Ibid., 195.
15. Ibid., 176.
16. George Seldes, *The Great Thoughts*, 104.

Chapter Six
Censorship U.S.A.

The First Amendment of the United States Constitution clearly protects freedom of speech and freedom of the press. As to the latter guarantee, it would seem that this would be to protect the American public from any underhanded government schemes, to warn us of any attempt to violate the Constitution or take over the country.

It would seem, though, that most of today's press (especially the electronic media) has voluntarily given up this right by serving as the tendentious tools or channels through which an endless stream of government propaganda is pumped into the minds of the public. However, this fact has already been stated earlier in this book, and there are other defined dangers to freedom of speech and thought. Isn't the college classroom supposed to be a forum for the communication and exchange of ideas and philosophies, a place where students can assimilate ideas and knowledge and come to their own conclusions about the nature of the world and the universe? This is currently being threatened by a conservative infiltration group known, paradoxically, as "Accuracy in Academia."

This organization, reputedly an offshoot of the Moral Majority (anyone surprised?), plants student spies in various classrooms in colleges and universities across the country, whose "duty" is to keep an eye on their professors and report any political theorizing or discussions that are out of context with the course being taught.

On March 5, 1986, a debate was held at the State University of Buffalo between John LeBoutillier, a former congressman and the unpaid president of Accuracy in Academia, and Bertell Ollman, professor of politics at New York University.

According to a newspaper article covering the debate, written by Charles Anzalone and published in the March 6, 1986, edition of the *Buffalo Evening News*, Mr. LeBoutillier claimed his group looks for the same things "60 Minutes" does every week on television, such as misrepresentation, abuses of power, and faulty information. Sounds like he ought to be looking in Washington, D.C., instead of college campuses, doesn't it?

Professor Ollman claimed that Accuracy in Academia is the latest example of McCarthyism, interested in attacking ideas it does not agree with and reducing college education to the sterility "of processed cheese."

Accuracy in Academia had been challenging professors at other universities across the country, accusing them of "liberal bias," and using the classroom to perpetuate their political beliefs. LeBoutillier said his group has attacked professors who have substituted their personal views for curriculum.

Professor Ollman contended that Accuracy in Academia has always criticized professors with liberal bias, and that the group's main interest is "in bias, not accuracy. And bias is those ideas they do not agree with."

Ollman also said that the organization is the latest expression of an immoral group "that has the audacity and mendacity to call itself the Moral Majority."

He called it a McCarthy-like group using McCarthy-like tactics and stated: "It's the threat that triggers conformity [on the campuses] as much as the actual act."

LeBoutillier countered by saying his group has been searching for conservative professors using the classroom to further their ideology.

"We still want to find instances of right-wing or very conservative classes to eliminate the biases that are thrown at us," LeBoutillier said.

About fifty demonstrators stood outside the Katherine Cornell Theatre (where the debate was held), holding signs and chanting anti–Accuracy in Academia slogans. The demonstrators did not object to Mr. LeBoutillier's right to speak, but opposed the purpose of Accuracy in Academia.

"We want to oppose [the group's] attempt to censor thought and to censor freedom of speech," said Peter Murphy, a graduate student involved in the demonstration. "We see it affecting all people."[1]

Will college professors who express their opinions and expound on their ideas be forced to drink hemlock a la Socrates?

The word *liberal* in *Webster's Dictionary* is defined as "favoring progress and reform in social institutions, and the fullest practicable liberty of individual action." Does this sound like the description of someone who would belong to Accuracy (?) in Academia, or describe in any way its purposes? One has to stifle a laugh at the president of this organization saying he wants to ferret out conservatives as well as liberals, when Accuracy in Academia is so obviously a right-wing setup. Why ferret out anybody, or interfere with the exchange of ideas in the classroom? It simply sounds like more Meddlemania.

Any repressive, censorship-oriented organization like Accuracy in Academia poses a serious threat to freethinking individuals everywhere. It represents a mentality that would like to limit choices and viewpoints and refuses to accept or acknowledge any opposition. If these people were to succeed in their course of action, we would soon see lollipops and ice-cream cones issued to college students on a daily basis, along with whatever intellectually sterile literature that could be found and deemed "nonsubversive," which would probably exclude 90 percent of all books ever written.

This kind of trend could lead to a situation where the following hypothetical article might appear in a campus newspaper:

Pompous State College
Campus Couple of the Month:
Dicky Purebread & Susie Twoshoes

Dicky is a model Pompous State student who plans on majoring in professional urine testing. He is also a full-time volunteer agent for the President's Committee on Subversive Campus Activities and has helped rid the campus of fifty-six left-wing student infiltrators, plus two professors with liberal leanings.

He is always in bed by 9 P.M., after stopping by the campus coffee shop to compare notes with other Subversive Activities agents, while they enjoy a rousing round of milk and cookies.

Susie likes to spend time reading Harlequin romance books when she isn't in classes or organizing campus morality rallies. She also keeps an eye on her professors to watch for any outbreaks of liberal behavior.

Dicky and Susie think that too much thinking or reading can be harmful because it might lead to disagreement with government policy or their elders.

Dicky says he thinks book burnings might be a good idea because there is too much subversive literature available.

He also suggests random breathalyzer testing in classrooms to make sure there aren't any student drinkers.

Dicky and Susie only go out together when a chaperone is available. Explains Susie, "Well, we're still young and impressionable and we both feel that someone should keep an eye on us."

When a chaperone is available, the threesome usually go to Dicky's dorm to watch tapes of "The Brady Bunch" and the "The Partridge Family" on the VCR in the lobby.

Says Dean of Students Horace Busybody, "I think students all over the country should emulate the wholesome example set by Dicky and Susie."

Censorship and Meddlemania have made their way onto college campuses, and things aren't looking too good.

And what about good old rock 'n' roll?

Over the years, rock 'n' roll music has ended up taking the blame for just about every problem there is, from juvenile delinquency and sexual promiscuity to drinking, drug abuse, and even teenage suicide.

COLLEGE STUDENT
OF
THE FUTURE

In the contemporary music field, there are hundreds of rock groups and performers who have produced exciting, delightful, and pleasing music.

Performers and groups like Elvis, the Beatles, the Rolling Stones, Jimi Hendrix, the Doors, Emerson, Lake & Palmer, Yes, Pink Floyd, the Who, Steppenwolf, Renaissance, Focus, Led Zeppelin, Deep Purple, and others too numerous to mention have provided a treasury of music that has given millions of people endless hours of listening pleasure.

The expression of the human spirit in the forms art and music has a special quality all of its own, and deserves few, if any, limitations.

How many great works of art or music have been destroyed or lost forever because of censorship and hypocrisy?

It is at the same time laughable and contemptible that so many meddlers seize on the rock music that a small minority of artists of questionable taste have produced, and use their material to attack the entire music industry.

It was just within the last year that a Congressional committee was commissioned to look into the possibility of instituting a rating system on rock 'n' roll records, an idea that is totally absurd and indicative of the petty mentality of today's "moral" crusaders.

An article in the March 6, 1986, edition of the *Buffalo Evening News* entitled, "First Lady Drummed Out of Rock Fest," describes how promoters of an antidrug rock concert pulled Nancy Reagan from the program because she wanted to turn the April 26 event into a debate about offensive lyrics and music censorship.

(Is there no end to this woman's meddling?)

Tony Verna and Hal Uplinger, the promoters of the concert, said they decided to withdraw their invitation because of requests by the first lady's office to eliminate some performers because of "offensive" lyrics on past recordings.

"We respect Mrs. Reagan's concern, but there will be no—I repeat—no prior censorship from the White House," Verna said in a statement. "The rock 'n' roll industry has always had a maverick, anti-establishment, creative bend that youngsters appreciate."

Verna said barring performers the first lady found offensive would be a form of censorship and an insult to entertainers who volunteered their time and talent.[2]

Another antirock meddler, who was indulging in some on-the-spot picketing while Congress was debating the pros and cons of record rating is a certain Pastor Fletcher A. Brothers, who hosts a "religious" TV show called "Come Fly With The Eagles"(?), which was recently renamed "Victory Today"(??).

This man also runs a "concentration camp" for teenagers in Lakemont, New York, bizarrely called "Freedom Village," and has distributed petitions all over the place calling for the banishment and censoring of the music and records of various heavy metal bands.

His premise for this is that the lyrics contained in some of the songs by these bands corrupt young people and cause them to commit suicide. As ridiculous as this sounds, this kind of thing has been going on for years. All kinds of religious fanatics and preachers have for years been condemning rock 'n' roll music as an "instrument of the devil," and blaming it for most of society's ills.

Now, it is a more or less accepted fact that most teenagers pass through some "rebellious" years in their search for self-discovery.

As trashy and vulgar as some of these groups might be, they probably wouldn't be so popular, or sell so many records, if they hadn't been made attractive in the eyes of young people because of the condemnation of these groups by fanatics and preachers. It's sort of like the "forbidden fruit" syndrome. By condemning these groups, these people only make them more attractive to the rebellious teen. And the simple fact is, after all, that music is just music—just an entertainment form.

To single out one facet of this entertainment form and build it up into a monstrous scapegoat for the problems of today is the act of an irrational mind. This tendency to single out situations, people, and objects, and build up a fire of exaggerated hysteria around them, is one of the basic techniques used by meddlers and would-be dictators to brainwash others and is reflected in the susceptibility of the masses to propaganda.

Nietzsche once composed an epigram that reads: "Madness is rare in individuals—but in groups, parties, nations and ages it is the rule."[3]

Many of the mass movements today are irrational in nature, springing from nebulous and prejudicial premises, and have been promulgated by pressure groups and individuals who are suffering from the misbegotten notion in this "free" country, their viewpoints are superior. Nowadays in this "free" country, we see censorship running rampant. Smoking is being banned in almost every place you go, drinking ages are being raised in most states. (Once again, "Adolf" Reagan threatened to withhold federal highways funds from states that refused to raise the legal drinking age. Now, if at eighteen a person can vote, get married, or get drafted and possibly end up getting killed in a war that someone else started, why should he have to wait until twenty-one to drink? This is just another hypocritical double-standard being enforced by the Meddlemaniacs, and is another example of the outrageousness being perpetrated in this country.)

Not only that; you have pressure groups trying to remove and ban "adult" magazines from stores, drug testing programs are being perpetrated against the public, mandatory seat belt laws are being passed "for our own good," alcoholic beverages are being banned from public parks, and government officials are attempting to keep more and more underhanded maneuvers under wraps.

The nature of our society and laws is changing from libertarian to draconian, and that can only spell disaster for the individual. This metamorphosis is occurring because meddlers, censors, and other self-appointed "guardians of morality" have taken advantage of the democratic nature of our republic and the freedoms guaranteed by our Constitution to interfere and restrict the rights, choices, and privacy of others, and to try to instill their values and social ideals as pre-eminent and predominant, out of some erroneous sense of moral superiority.

A simple example of hypocrisy and censorship on an everyday level is the way feature-length movies are edited for television. Every day, on the streets, on the job, in the schools—just about anywhere that people come into contact with each other—expletives are commonly heard and used.

The way dialogues in many movie scripts are written, the occasional use of profanity helps to emphasize a character or story line. Even when such words are bleeped over, or an "acceptable" word voiced over (e.g., darn or frig), most people know what the word is that is being glossed over.

So what is the point of editing out or glossing over "unacceptable" words?

As discussed in chapter three, censorship can also be found in the forms of dress codes and rules governing the way a person wears his hair.

As long as somebody does his or her job and is reasonable and cooperative, what does it matter or what business is it of anyone else what a person wears, or how long or short his or her hair is?

One motive behind this is to restrain individual self-expression. The other causes are simply based on Pilgrimlike prejudice and intolerance.

Some people are so absolutely convinced that their way is the right way, they won't hesitate to demand conformity to their ways and practices.

The more they say it and preach it, the more they believe it—they inject themselves with the opium of their own words, until they are so convinced of the rightness of their cause or position that there is no way of reasonably communicating with them.

Unfortunately, they also narcotize a lot of gullible and naive people who don't know how to think for themselves.

Now let's face it, the only way freedom of speech and thought, and artistic expression, can be preserved is if censorship is kept to a bare minimum.

Recently, a local TV station in Buffalo, New York, ran the movie *Caddyshack* on their late show, and the censor's shears had been at work again, this time having been influenced by the treacherous "war on drugs." At one point in the movie Lacy

Underall (portrayed by actress Cindy Morgan) tells Ty Webb (portrayed by actor Chevy Chase) that she enjoys going to bullfights on acid. This was notably missing from the whitewashed version, no doubt because it was "inappropriate."

Almost every aspect and area of personal behavior today is being subjected to some form of censorship.

On the college campus, in rock 'n' roll, movies, television, magazines, books (some books advertised in inserts in publications like *TV Guide* have Xs marked on them as warnings, which probably really only makes them more attractive to minors), and even in stores and public places.

It would seem that the leading advocates of censorship are basically interested in defining "American" morality, and what the "right" things are.

However, since this nation is made up of diverse individuals, with diverse viewpoints and beliefs, all these censorship-oriented movements are vain and detrimental crusades that will only irritate and injure millions of people.

After all, man's inhumanity to man does not come just in the forms of Inquisitions and totalitarian practices, it also comes in the forms of intolerance, prejudice, and censorship.

The famous lawyer Clarence S. Darrow (1857–1938) once said, "You can only protect your liberties in this world by protecting the other man's freedom. You can only be free if I am free."[4]

Maybe this is something all censorship-minded Meddlemaniacs should ponder.

NOTES

1. Charles Anzalone, "Debate on Accuracy in Academia Reveals Biases," *Buffalo Evening News* (March 6, 1986), B5.
2. "First Lady Drummed Out Of Rock Fest," *Buffalo Evening News*, (reprinted from UPI) (March 6, 1986), A5.
3. Friedrich Nietzsche, *Beyond Good and Evil* (New York: Vintage Books/Random House, Inc., 1966). 90.
4. George Seldes, *The Great Thoughts*, 100.

Chapter Seven
Drugs and Alcohol

Despite all the antidrug garbage being spewed out nowadays in the manufactured media campaign called the "war on drugs," the fact remains that drugs have been around on the planet for thousands of years, and the vast majority of people who use them today are not adversely affected by them, do not need "treatment," and do not believe they are doing anything wrong.

In the year 3400 B.C., the Chinese emperor Shen Nung wrote a pharmacopeia (a pharmaceutical guidebook) that recommended marijuana as a cure-all drug for everything from headaches to the gout.[1] This means that marijuana has been in use on the planet for over fifty-three centuries. Why is it all of a sudden considered "dangerous?"

Marijuana is also known to cure and arrest glaucoma, and is also used by many cancer patients to alleviate the side effects of anticancer therapies such as nausea and vomiting.[2]

According to a news program broadcast within the last year, some senior citizens in California, who were suffering from severe arthritic pain, were injected with cocaine, and were completely relieved and able to walk about and even dance without any difficulty.

So, it should be obvious already that all the propaganda denouncing such drugs as "dangerous" is 99 percent false—just manufactured media hype.

No matter what the self-righteous moralists and politicians say, millions of people think of smoking a joint as being no better or worse than having a glass of beer or a shot of scotch.

Now what is the basic problem with drugs? The problem is they are "illegal" and cost a lot of money to get.

Who is usually considered a victim of drug abuse? Usually someone who spends all his money on a particular drug to support his habit.

Why are they so expensive? Because the government, in its infinite foolishness, has passed "laws" making them illegal, thereby perpetuating a long-term Prohibition-type situation that is an on-running gold mine for organized crime.

Now, before Prohibition was enacted (the Eighteenth Amendment), organized crime as such operated on a much smaller scale, with prostitution and gambling as the main sources of illegal revenue. But when Prohibition was inflicted on the American public, a virtual fountain of gold opened up for the underworld, and gave them the financial power to grow to the level of being almost a second government.

As Peter Maas put it in *The Valachi Papers*:

> Racketeering did not begin to be a national force until the 1920's.
>
> Prohibition, of course, was the catalyst. In addition to those old standbys—prostition and gambling—there was now a new illicit commodity that millions of Americans craved: alcohol.
>
> And it brought the racketeer riches and respectability beyond his wildest dreams; in effect most of the nation became his accomplice.[3]

Now, it should be obvious that in respect to drugs, organized crime is still raking in billions of tax-free dollars, thanks to the stupid and myopic antidrug laws on the books.

The government claims that the underworld annually yanks in $110 billion a year from the drug trade.[4]

If business like this is going on, it is because millions of people enjoy using drugs, and there is a big demand for them.

All those untaxed billions wouldn't be going to line the pockets of murderers and thieves if we weren't suffering from unrealistic laws and the personal prejudices of the meddlers. According to NORML, in 1985, America's marijuana harvest produced a record crop of $18.6 billion, putting it slightly ahead of corn ($18.5 billion) as the most valuable crop in the nation.

"The fact that an illegal crop is the most valuable crop in the United States is another indication of troubles in our farm economy," claimed Kevin Zeese, NORML national director. "With our country over two trillion dollars in debt, it is time for us to tax America's most valuable crop."

Obviously, these are sound words of advice that the entire country could benefit from.

The glaring fact here is that the chief beneficiary of antidrug laws is organized crime—not the public—and every day that these "laws" are in effect, organized crime continues to get richer and richer.

With this in mind, you have to wonder why our elected officials refuse to see reason.

Is it simply a case of personal prejudice and Meddlemania versus practical reality? Or is it possible that many of these antidrug crusaders are actually on the mob's payroll, since the racketeers would have the strongest reason to keep certain drugs illegal? Of course, it's not just the mob that has a vested interest in keeping illegal drugs illegal; there are also the big, international drug (pharmaceutical) cartels and the liquor industry.

Now if marijuana were legal and someone suffering from a headache could smoke a joint instead of taking an aspirin (and get a pleasant "buzz" in the bargain), wouldn't you imagine that aspirin sales would drop off shortly? And who would be the loser in such a situation? Why, the aspirin manufacturer, of course. And here is something they don't tell you when they're trying to push all this antidrug hoopla down your throat: according to a report released by the General Accounting Office, prescription drugs are responsible for 74 percent of all deaths attributed to drug overdose. Seventy-five percent of all hospital-related drug emergencies are caused by the use of prescription drugs.[5] Gee, you probably thought that pot and coke were responsible for all that kind of stuff, didn't you?

And as far as booze goes, think about this: if people smoked a joint after work instead of going to the bar for a beer or a whiskey, then the liquor manufacturers would end up losing money on the deal. Both the drug cartels and the distillers realize this, and one of the last things they want to see is the legalization of marijuana or any other drug that might cut into their profits or threaten their position.

The most reasonable and intelligent course would be to legalize the sale and use of marijuana, and sell it through state or federally licensed package stores (the same way hard liquor is sold in most states). This way, each sale could be taxed, and the vast tax revenues generated from the legal sale of marijuana could go toward alleviating our huge national debts. Also, the customer would have a better selection to choose from and presumably cheaper prices, and organized crime would lose a great deal of tax-free illicit income.

When you consider the fact that one of the deadliest drugs of all, alcohol, is freely available to adults almost everywhere in the country, while less harmful substances such as marijuana are kept illegal, and their users victimized, you have to wonder what kind of hypocritical double-dealing is going on.

Alcohol causes irreversible physical damage, such as cirrhosis of the liver and permanent destruction of brain cells.

But, except for a few "dry" counties in some states, this drug can be purchased almost anywhere in the United States, in a variety of forms (beer, wine, cordials, whiskey, vodka, gin, et cetera).

Despite all the clamor stirred up by the meddlers and the media about drugs, and the misinformation they have dispensed, let's take a look at marijuana-use and substance-abuse policies in the Netherlands.

Marijuana use was decriminalized there in 1976 with the Amendment of the Opium Act.

Cannabis has been sold in cafés and youth centers there since 1978. As a result, drug use has actually dropped off and considerably so. In a nationwide survey in the Netherlands done in 1986, 12 percent of people aged fifteen to twenty-four had tried marijuana at least once, 5 percent currently smoked once a month, and 1.6 percent smoked once every three days.

In direct contrast to that, in a survey of American youth done by the University of Michigan's "Monitoring the Future" program, 54 percent of all teenagers have tried pot by age eighteen, 25.9 percent smoked at least once a month, and 5 percent smoked at least once every three days.

NORML, after comparing the Dutch and Ann Arbor (University of Michigan) statistics, made the obvious conclusion:

> These studies raise serious questions about the assumption that the marijuana laws protect our youth.
>
> The reality is that marijuana prohibition may hurt our children by glamorizing a forbidden fruit, encouraging sale in the schools, blocking communication in the family, and making information about marijuana seem like war propaganda.[6]

To quote writer Mark Swain:

> By keeping marijuana illegal and stigmatizing its youthful smokers as natural-born life-long miscreants and criminal sociopaths, the American law-enforcement system effectively provides troubled adolescents with a perfect symbol of anti-authoritarian sentiment through which to work out their fantasies of outlawry and rebellion.[7]

Not only do our ridiculous antidrug laws make "criminals" out of otherwise honest, law-abiding citizens, a great many individual lives have been disrupted and destroyed by them.

How many professional athletes and sports figures have had their careers ended because traces of drugs showed up in an unconstitutional urine test?

Supposedly some of the New England Patriots were using drugs during the 1986 Super Bowl game against the Chicago Bears. So what?

Many of these hardworking athletes just want to catch a "buzz" and enjoy their success without being harassed by self-righteous busybodies.

Unfortunately, they have become victims of the MPA (Meddler Police Action), and their individual freedom of choice has more or less been extorted from them.

How many hardworking employees have lost their jobs or been railroaded needlessly into "treatment" programs because of all the hysterical propaganda generated by the media and this despicable drug-testing business?

It would seem that the American public has forgotten all about the McCarthy Red Scare and the Salem witch-hunts. It definitely looks like the "historical amnesia" that Ovid Demaris mentioned has set in again.

Once again, the American public is being victimized by another ruthless witch-hunt, and this time around, drugs are the political cow chip to be kicked around and made a stink of.

What is really unbelievable is that most of these antidrug people have never even tried any drugs, and have absolutely no firsthand experience. It's like saying you don't like venison and can't stand it without ever having tried any. Now how can anyone who has never tried something know for sure, without a doubt, that something is no good? Because they've been told so by "experts"? We've already seen what experts can be made of, as detailed in chapter two.

It definitely seems that a more lucid and thorough appraisal of the marijuana issue, as well as other important issues, is in order.

"The Report by the President's Commission on Organized Crime," which recommends police-state tactics and stiffening of laws, is like "The Meese Commission's Report on Pornography," mostly a collection of errors, hysterical misinformation, and outright lies that are designed to support the prudish, self-righteous attitudes, and "moral" values of the people who wrote them. And, of course, the hypocrisy that is so typical of many a Meddlemaniac came to the surface when the deputy director of the commission, Rodney Smith, was asked to provide a sample of urine for a Congressional committee. He refused.

Rep. Gary L. Ackerman (D-NY), who requested the sample, remarked, "I thank you for very eloquently proving the point we have set out to prove."[8]

Rep. Patricia Schroeder (D-CO) called the urine testing idea "idiotic" and "an embarrassment."[9]

Ira Glasser of the ACLU said, "Instead of waging war against criminals, the President's commission proposes to wage war against innocent American citizens."[10]

Several newspapers who have retained their integrity also opposed the report. The *New York Times* went as far as to recommend the legalization of marijuana. The *Washington Times* called the recriminalization of marijuana a "folly." The *Philadelphia Inquirer* said it was out of step with the trends in the states.[11]

Other newspapers who editorially opposed the report were The *Washington Post*, The *Baltimore Sun*, The *Boston Globe*, The *Portland Oregonian*, and The *Wall Street Journal*.[12]

Fortunately, not everyone is sleeping or suffering from "amnesia," as can be seen from the facts provided. The liberal drug policy enacted in the Netherlands has actually reduced drug consumption among teenagers and adults, while allowing greater latitude in the area of individual freedom of choice.

In this country, however, an archaic and despicable phenomenon has arisen to combat teenage drug "abuse": "concentration camps" for young people. These bizarre places seem to be springing up all over the country, and have been openly advocated by the media via the trashy, propagandistic 1985 CBS TV-movie titled *Not My Kid*. This piece of film garbage included all the usual heavily embellished "facts" and hysterical lies one would expect nowadays. A more appropriate title for this film would have been "The Manchurian Candidate Meets the Gestapo."

We see in this program the same brainwashing techniques used by Sun Myung Moon to subvert the minds of thousands of young people: isolation from reality and the outside world, strict discipline and regimentation, "love-bombing," and plenty of guilt-inducing accusations and browbeating.

Of course, near the end of the picture, when the principal character, a teenage girl, has "seen the light" and been "cured," she follows through with the obligatory slow-motion dash across the room to hug mommy and daddy. And then, at the end of the picture, arch-meddler Nancy Reagan appears and recommends several antidrug books as a follow-up assignment to the program.

Of course, the harsh practices of these real-life "schools" were glossed over in the movie.

In reality, the young victims of these places, after being forced to "tell all" and "bare their souls," are then bossed around, beaten, humiliated, and treated like criminals, as well as having their mail censored. (That's right, this kind of stuff really goes on in "the land of the free.")

You would think in an age as supposedly enlightened as this these kinds of practices would not be tolerated, especially with examples like the Netherlands policy to fall back on.

Just the fact that such archaic and cruel practices are still being perpetuated today shows that, in spite of all or acquired knowledge and technology, understanding and true insight are in short supply, and society is stagnating in a cesspool of self-righteousness, intolerance, and hypocrisy.

As far as drug legislation goes, reforms are what is needed, not recriminalization or totalitarian practices.

Marijuana should be legalized, sold, and taxed for the benefit of the American economy and the freedom of choice of those who wish to smoke it.

Possession of small amounts of euphoric drugs, like hashish and cocaine, should be decriminalized—and truly dangerous drugs like heroin and PCP should remain the targets of law-enforcement agencies like the DEA.

Those who do not wish to take drugs don't have to; nobody's twisting their arm or holding a gun to their head. And those who do should not have their freedom of choice interfered with by Meddlemaniacs and law and order dictators.

Of course, in a way, democratic procedures and practices in this country have become comparable to a constant psychological and ideological exercise in sadomasochism: the right gets into office and attacks the left—the left gets into office and attacks the right; there always seems to be a gaping void as far as any kind of bipartisan coexistence is concerned, except when it benefits politicians personally to go along with the same thing, especially in an election year.

Obviously, considering that organized crime supposedly yanks in $110 billion a year from drug trafficking, it is absolute lunacy to keep on propagating unrealistic laws when a large section of the public is opposed to them, and other countries like Holland are living proof that legalization works.

What has to be remembered is that we are faced with an "unholy trinity" (organized crime, drug cartels, and the liquor industry), that wants to stand in the way of rationality and lucidity to preserve their positions and riches. And they are being aided by a lot of narrow-minded morons who actively spread a lot of superstitious misinformation about drugs. One of the most popular myths that has been promoted is the association of drug use with occultism and devil worship. A lot of people (mostly "religious" leaders) have attempted to link drugs with occult practices; they have attempted to portray drugs as an agent that leads people into the practices of witchcraft and satanism.

Now, in reality, probably less than 5 percent of the drug-taking public are actually involved in occult areas. And as anyone who knows anything about the occult will tell you, it is not so much marijuana or cocaine that are used in magical or satanic rituals, but an array of more obscure, esoteric substances. As Richard Cavendish points out: "One formula for summoning devils requires the burning of coriander, hemlock, parsley, liquor of black poppy, fennel, sandalwood and henbane. Fumes from burning henbane can cause convulsions and temporary insanity."[13]

And, in quoting a description of a black mass from J. K. Huysman's novel *La Bas*, Cavendish writes: "For incense they burn rue, myrtle, dried nightshade, henbane and the powerful narcotic thorn-apple."[14]

Now, when was the last time you heard of anyone getting busted for dealing in henbane, thorn-apple or liquor of black poppy? All this outcry over drugs is reminiscent of a line from Shakespeare's play "Hamlet": "The lady doth protest too much, methinks."

As discussed in chapter two, the public is constantly bombarded every day with antidrug media spots, with plenty of celebrities giving little antidrug speeches.

One of these, the "Cocaine—the Big Lie" campaign, which features ex-football star Mercury Morris, is one of the more regularly shown ones. Now, the only "big lie" here is the idea that cocaine is as bad as the government would have you believe. They don't get any tax dollars from the sale of cocaine (because it's against the "law"), and so now they are trying to brainwash the American public with all this nonsense.

No doubt a lot of our tax dollars are probably going to pay off these celebrities in the announcements. And then you have plenty of volunteers on TV talk shows—the usual assortment of weaklings and crybabies who feel compelled to humiliate themselves in public by confessing their "faults" and, in between a lot of sobbing and sniffling, going on and on about the "horrors" of their drug "experiences." This encourages many gullible viewers to think of themselves as naughty children who need to be guided and corrected by their "parents" (i.e., government officials and other assorted meddlers and would-be dictators).

In this respect, many Americans could be compared to spoiled, self-indulgent, and apathetic children who, surrounded by toys (material comforts and devices) and having no volition or respect for freedom, allow their "parents" to make all their decisions and govern all their moves.

Now, in early October of 1986, the Reagan Administration was discovered to have been deliberately conducting a misinformation campaign about Libya and the government of Muammar Qaddafi, which resulted in the resignation of State Department spokesman Bernhard Kalb. If the government is willing to spread lies and propaganda in one area, why wouldn't they do it in every area?

The same commission report that recommends turning America into a police state also suggests dividing the nation—turning neighbor against neighbor, friend against friend, children against parents—all the treacherous and despicable practices that could have been found in Nazi Germany.

The report states: "it is our obligation to look further and recognize among us—friends, relatives, colleagues, and other 'respectable' people—are the driving force of the "assault on our country."[15]

Such an outrageous suggestion should raise goose pimples on the skin of every individual.

In October 1986, a radio broadcast announced that New York governor Mario Cuomo (who also had a hand in New York's ridiculous seat belt laws), had established a toll-free "Judas" line for people to turn in suspected drug users or dealers.

Of course, you won't get thirty pieces of silver, but you will have the satisfaction of knowing you helped to promote totalitarianism in America.

Rumor has it that you also are sent a painting depicting Judas receiving his thirty pieces of silver, which is personally autographed by the governor.

It is absolute insanity for millions of hardworking, honest citizens to be made "criminals" of by outdated, absurd antidrug laws. As with marijuana, if cocaine was legal and cheap, individual usage would probably drop off, less people would die from overdoses and poisoned supplies, and hundreds of thousands of people would avoid having their lives wrongfully disrupted and destroyed by the Meddlemaniacs and law-enforcement enthusiasts.

Now let's take a look at the way it really is.

The government and other assorted meddlers scream about drug abuse, while alcohol (one of the deadliest drugs of all) is freely available just about anywhere in the United States.

They howl about the immorality of gambling and underworld "numbers" or policy rackets, while at the same time, most states run lotteries and operate off-track horse-betting parlors.

You could be watching some spurious antidrug announcement on TV, and right after that, on would come a beer or wine cooler ad.

Despite the fact that hordes of intelligent, sensible people from all walks of life have advocated the legalization of marijuana and the reform of other drug laws, we are still faced with idiotic holdouts who refuse to see reason and want to continue to terrorize and brainwash the American public.

Either it's their personal prejudices getting in the way or else they're on the payroll of one or more members of the "unholy trinity," which wants to keep on perpetuating the "illegality" of certain drugs.

Obviously, this situation is not going to improve unless more peole throw off this yoke of misinformation and untruths, and demand that our so-called "leaders" snap out of this totalitarian delirium and come to terms with reality.

And after the proper reforms have been made, these political and social extremists should be whisked off to the nearest Meddlemania Withdrawal Center for comprehensive treatment.

NOTES

1. Norman Taylor, *Narcotics* (New York: Dell Books, 1970), 20–21.
2. Article appearing in *The Leaflet*, (April 1986), 6.
3. Peter Maas, *The Valachi Papers* (New York: Bantam Books, Inc., 1968), 83.
4. Article appearing in *The Leaflet*, 1.
5. "Activist Facts," *High Times* magazine, (December 1986), page 29.
6. "Kids in Holland Spurn Legal Pot," Mark Swain, *High Times* magazine, (August 1986), 23.
7. Ibid., 24.
8. Quote from Rep. Gary Ackerman (D-NY) appearing in *The Leaflet*, p.
9. Ibid., 8.
10. Ibid., 8.
11. Ibid., 8.
12. Ibid., 8.
13. Richard Cavendish, *The Black Arts* (New York: G. P. Putnam and Sons, Inc., 1967), 267.
14. Ibid., 366.
15. Quote from report by The President's Commission on Organized Crime appearing in *The Leaflet*, 8.

Chapter Eight
A Short Treatise on Iconoclastic Principles

The time has come to scrap tradition and established custom and thought, and move ahead with bold new concepts in every area of human existence.

Too long have we been burdened with sacred cows and plastic idols that have allowed repressive and unreasonable policies and schools of thought to dominate our culture.

We have too many people around who want to perpetuate "the good old days" and "old fashioned values"—people who want to maintain the same old rigid status quo, and who want to keep our culture in an arrested state of development.

It's time to say we've had enough—enough of these impostors who say they stand for freedom and liberty but instead perpetrate totalitarian practices and oppressive "laws" and policies on the sovereign citizens of this great nation.

Nothing good in the way of change or progress has every come from sticking to tradition or "old-fashioned" values.

The shackles of technocracy, pseudomoralism, and religious hokum have to be cast off before any serious reforms or progress can be made.

Too many good people have been victimized or made criminals of because of the cheap, ridiculous, self-righteous prejudices and attitudes of so-called "good, patriotic, moral" people and the absurd and hypocritical "laws" that the pompous blowhards and sanctimonious windbags in government office have passed.

It is not only the immediate, present-day freedoms that are in danger, it is the freedoms down the line in the next centuries that are in peril as well.

No doubt, the people behind this current outbreak of right-wing extremism and "religious" fanaticism must have a blueprint for long-range America in mind, sort of their own version of a thousand-year Reich for this country, one stained indelibly with the foul odors of self-righteousness, hypocrisy, and sanctimoniousness. Where people like this come up with such shameless gall and vicious intolerance God only knows. But let's face it—to be able to live free and make choices and adult decisions, to live one's life the way one chooses, is rapidly becoming a thing of the past.

This period in American history should probably be remembered as a dark time when Reaganism was running rampant and corporate dictators, religious impersonators, and intolerant moralizers almost succeeded in turning the greatest free nation into a police state, threatening our very Constitution and the freedom of choice and self-expression of every citizen.

These censorship-oriented attempts to stifle the freedom of choice and self-expression of the citizenry are reminiscent of the Cultural Revolution in Red China, which wiped out artistic expression and intellectual freedom for nearly a decade.

Every time progress in the field of individual freedom moves forward and seems to be taking hold, along comes control-conscious and censorship-oriented busybodies who do everything they can to destroy this progress.

The situation could be compared to a soufflé that is baking in the oven, carefully prepared, rising to perfection, and then along come the meddlers to slam the oven door and POW!—it's all over for the soufflé.

It would seem that now, more than ever, firm steps must be taken to keep the premium on the individual and individual rights and freedom of choice, before they are gobbled up by technocracy and Meddlemania.

Nowadays, people without an original thought in their heads or anything really serious to say are trying to call the shots in every department. And if the American public stopped taking them seriously and believing everything they said and thought about how preposterous their pseudo-ideologies and social proposals were, they would probably wonder how they could have ever allowed themselves to be so gullible and stupid.

Now, basically, a lot of this bamboozlement is made possible because so many people become enamored with icons.

An icon is generally accepted as being a cherished institution or belief; the name was originally applied to the religious statuary seen on altars in churches, primarily Catholic churches.

In today's world, the term *icon* could be used to describe a wide variety of things—from established traditions and customs to outstanding figures in certain fields of endeavor.

"Uncle Sam" is an icon—a contrived symbol used to supposedly epitomize the spirit of this country.

The American flag is an icon—it symbolizes the unity of the fifty states represented by the fifty stars.

Mickey Mantle is an icon—to many people, he represents the idyll of what a baseball player should be.

The problem starts when icons become vehicles for manipulation. For example: the recruitment posters that feature pictures of "Uncle Sam" pointing out at the viewer with the message overhead reading: "Uncle Sam Wants You!"

Who in the world *is* Uncle Sam?

In this case, it is the people in power, who have probably started a war somewhere and want to con you into risking your life fighting in it.

A great many icons are deliberately contrived and promoted as a means of coaxing and convincing people to do things willingly that they normally would not want any part of.

This is where the concept of the iconoclast comes in today, at least as far as being a tool to help individuals remain individuals, and avoid being deceived by misinformation and nonsense.

Iconoclast means "image-breaker," and is a general term for anyone who challenges cherished beliefs or ideas.

The term was originally applied to the Vikings when they invaded Norway in the tenth century and, when sacking and looting villages, would break into the churches and smash the religious statuary (the icons) with their clubs.

The concept here is to restrain the urge to take things at face value, and subject to the harshest scrutiny whatever remotely resembles an icon, and, should it prove itself to be a spurious vehicle for manipulation and propaganda, dispose of it on the scrap heap. Many people seem to cling to icons as anchors with which to keep themselves fastened to reality.

But there is no substitute for truth, and many icons are used to spread lies and falsehoods.

People used to believe that the world was flat until an iconoclast named Christopher Columbus proved otherwise.

As long as we are burdened with icons and contemporary mythology conjured up by government officials and Meddlemaniacs, there will always be a need for for iconoclastic individuals who are willing to challenge the status quo and smash the sacred cows erected by the iconographers. "Americans" are supposedly (according to the way that TV shows portray them) the shrewdest, most intelligent, most affluent people on the face of the earth, while, paradoxically, at the same time, fanatically law-abiding and intolerant of any "wrongdoing," eagerly supportive of the idiotic policies originating in Washington, D.C., and somehow just naturally superior to citizens of any other country.

The media icons have used the public's trust in them to promote a lot of nationalism-oriented nonsense, trying to convince the people that it is in their best interest to accept unconstitutional police-state tactics and practices.

Everybody has his or her own idea of what patriotism is. To me it means to be proud of being a member of a nation unique on the face of the earth for its industriousness, diversity of cultures, and great achievements.

Unfortunately, it seems that today you aren't considered to be a patriot unless you bow to the slavemasters in Washington, D.C., as you mindlessly mouth ignorant slogans like, "America—love it or leave it," while nibbling on a slice of apple pie and waving a flag.

Instead of retreating into the refuges of society and "religion," new frontiers and pathways need to be sought out and discovered to keep the human intellect and spirit operating at peak efficiency.

It seems that the politicians and "religious" leaders behind all this right-wing authoritarian nonsense want to stop the sociocultural clock and maintain the same musty status quo forever.

It seems that what we need is an iconoclastic, cultural, and ideological renaissance in order to eject stale and outdated concepts, lifestyles, and ideas that are causing atrophy of the human spirit. Otherwise, we will end up with generation after generation of puppets and saps, ready to goose-step upon command.

Chapter Nine
A Concluding Discussion

After reviewing the preceding pages of this book, and analyzing and assimilating the facts, references, and quotes contained therein, it should be obvious that America is still under the hangover of prejudicial Pilgrimlike attitudes and ways of thinking, and personal freedom is still as much in danger as it ever was.

Underneath the glittering facade of space-age technology, there still lurks all the dark superstitions and schools of thought that have threatened the individual since the dawn of man's existence. Our buildings and inventions may have progressed to a high degree, yet people haven't really changed that much. And this fact alone will always be a major stumbling block to anyone who would be truly free.

As long as we have "religions" that preach fear, guilt, and submission instead of self-discovery and freedom, as long as we have corporations that actively try to enslave their employees and practice police state tactics on them, as long as we have governments who use the "law" and legality to manipulate, suppress, and control the masses, and perpetrate unconstitutional legislation that they selfishly desire—the way to individuality and liberty will always be paved with hardships and unjust interference from meddlers and dictators. Knowledge itself is unobjective, the pure and simple facts. It is up to the individual to decipher and interpret that knowledge and come to specific conclusions.

This is extremely difficult to do where censorship exists (a blatant form of hypocrisy) and where "moral" values and social ideals are dictated and enforced by a self-appointed group of would-be elitists who consider themselves to be superior to their fellow men.

The American public and mankind in general are being sold down the river by self-righteous opportunists and would-be dictators. The concept behind our Constitution and the Bill of Rights was that all men should have the opportunity to live their lives as they see fit, to think, what they wish to think and express themselves in truth and action without censorship or suppression by governments or religions.

Man's history is rife with examples of censorship, tyranny, and innumerable accounts of human rights violations.

The current administration decries human rights violations in foreign countries, but seems to be doing its best to trim away and violate ours every day.

It should be quite obvious that the government is grossly overstepping its bounds, and freedom itself could soon become an extinct species unless people start waking up.

Webster's Dictionary defines *fascism* as "a strongly nationalistic regime characterized by regimentation, rigid censorship and suppression of opposition."

The same book defines *tyranny* as "unrestrained exercise of power; unmerciful rule."

Standing back and looking at the big picture, at the way the Reagan Administration and a host of other political impostors are operating, it would seem that we are witnessing tyrannical fascism in action, a syndrome that rapidly develops into totalitarianism if not checked in its incipient stages.

Why is this unnoticed or misunderstood by the public? Because, as usual, the political dictators have been aided and abetted by their co-conspirators (e.g., "experts," "religious" leaders, and corporate "land barons") who relentlessly work to mislead and deceive the people. And it isn't all that tough to do, since they usually have human nature and social training and submissiveness in their favor. From kindergarten up, the masses are taught to respect and bow to authority and defer to and obey the "laws of the land," no matter how stupid, unrealistic, or un-American these "laws" might be. This is where the "give 'em

A GOOSE-STEPPING SAP

an inch and they'll take a mile" type of thinking comes into play.

It's sort of like murder; the first time it might be hard to commit, but each successive murder becomes easier and easier to pull off. If government officials are allowed to go on and on perpetrating police state tactics and policing the American public, it won't be too long before there won't be any distinguishable differences between the U.S.A. and the USSR

A recent situation already foreshadows that. In the last week of 1986, approximately fifty Soviet émigrés that had sought sanctuary in this country decided to return to Russia. When interviewed on TV, one of the émigrés remarked that for various reasons, he "couldn't see where the U.S. was that much freer a country than Russia." Quite a sorry state of affairs, don't you think?

The founding fathers of this country intended this country to be isolationist, to mind its own business and stay out of the affairs of other countries.

No doubt they must be turning over in their graves to see that America is involved in the affairs of almost every country on the face of the earth, has supported and is supporting dictatorial regimes for "political" reasons (birds of a feather?), and is rapidly becoming the kind of country they left because of tyranny and human rights abuses.

Laughably enough, a current series of CBS-TV spots titled "We the People" features different celebrities boasting of the supremacy of individual rights, while, at the same time in reality, these rights are being violated every day.

The progressive spirits of invention, exploration, experimentation, and individualism are being slowly extinguished by the malicious attempts of right-wing pressure groups, government officials, and pseudoreligious moralizers to establish a lily-white, censorship-oriented society.

The softness of the American public, the lack of REAL moral greatness that allows totalitarian practices, "househusbands," most so-called situation comedies, and the constant glorification of the police and the "law" on TV—in the place of original ideas, doctrines promoting freedom and honest portraits of men with real character—is part of the reason for the decline of freedom and the popularity of mindless prejudice.

While people are worrying about what kind of car to buy, or consulting psychiatrists over trauma they are suffering because a pet cat or dog won't eat its food, our personal liberties are about to take a nose dive down the toilet.

The truly free individual, who thinks for himself and has no interest in flag-waving rituals or blind nationalistic fervor, has his interest in the exploration and development of the inner man and his spiritual self.

Enough of these presumptuous little people with narrow, little minds, whose idea of spirituality is enforcing "laws" on others and living by antiquated ideas and standards.

Life is hard enough for those of us who have to work every day, without having to fend off meddlers and busybodies of all kinds. Instead of developing their own potential and minding their own business, too many people waste their time trying to impede and govern the lives of others.

Should we live like cowards and allow these self-righteous aggressors every opportunity to defile us and steal our honor and dignity, or will we stand up and fight like every freedom-loving man and woman has been forced to throughout the centuries, not only out of necessity, but also for the principle?

The development and freedom of each individual should be the primary consideration. Anyone who opposes this is an enemy of free will, freedom, and individual choice.

Why would anyone go to such much trouble to mislead and control others? Well, it should be obvious that what our so-called "leaders" want is to replace our constitutional society with a fascist oligarchy, under whose rule, freedom of choice, morality, and individual liberty will be restricted, defined, and controlled by a handful of totalitarian elitists.

Surely the allure of the idea of controlling absolutely such an industrialized and technologically developed super state that America is has got to be overpowering to such people. And, of course, the news media has done little to help. Instead of attacking these smug bureaucrats who lie and speak in riddles, they pamper them and encourage them instead of challenging them, thereby encouraging the public to believe in them.

The national situation could almost be compared to that of Louisiana under the governorship of Huey Long, who through relentless manipulation of the masses and the passage of one self-serving law after another almost managed to make himself the absolute dictator of that state.

In other words, in their way of thinking, it is okay to do immoral things or hurt other people, just as long as you have the official seal of approval. And if you happen to be in government office or hold high position, and if you happen to be afflicted with Meddlemania or the Snoopy Sniffer Syndrome, just think of all the wonderful ways you could meddle in other peoples lives and destroy those who disagree with you or oppose you.

It seems that the sole reason for many of these people to seek public office is that they have a bee in their bonnet and want to do some stinging.

However, these exclusive members of the School of Hypocrisy don't want to admit that rigidity, conformity, and censorship should be viewed as enemies of individual development and agents of intellectual and spiritual destruction.

The Reagan administration and all other government officials who advocate totalitarian and unconstitutional practices should be unceremoniously booted out of office, after first apologizing to the American public on national TV.

Life should be a rich feast to be savored and enjoyed, not a paranoid, starved existence where limits and roadblocks of all kinds are constantly being thrown in one's path by Meddlemaniacs and Snoopy Sniffers.

It is about time that we stopped letting our intelligences be insulted by the lies and nonsense that the media and our so-called "leaders" are always dispensing.

The political impostors, corporate dictators, and other assorted enemies of true liberty may have decided that they have won the ball game, but they cannot withstand the wrath of several hundred million sovereign citizens.

The time has come for all free-thinking, free-spirited individuals to take whatever steps are necessary to preserve what freedoms and liberties we still possess and win back those we've lost before the would-be dictators and spiritual morons succeed in destroying our birthrights.

Basically, these people need to be slapped hard and told in no uncertain terms that what the people of this country do is NONE OF THEIR BUSINESS.

For the sake of our freedom, our children's freedom, and their children's children's freedom, we must nip these repressive practices in the bud immediately.

So what does it all come down to? Learn to say: "No!"

"No!"—to repressive or unconstitutional "laws" or programs.

"No!"—to people who try to dictate morality.

"No!"—to anyone who would try to interfere with your personal life and freedoms.

Here are some added suggestions for improving these conditions:

1) Automatic fines for any government official who attempts to dictate morality or attempts to introduce or pass any "moral" legislation (at least five thousand dollars per offense).
2) Mandatory jail sentences for any politician or corporate official caught trying to implement practices like urine testing (at least ten years).
3) News programs should be required to present both sides of all issues, not just the sides Washington wants the public to see.
4) The appointment of impartial observers to act as "watchdog" groups to keep an eye on all bureaucrats and polticians.
5) Repeal of all oppressive and unconstitutional "laws" currently on the books.
6) Legalization of marijuana and decriminalization for the possession of small amounts of euphoric drugs like hashish and cocaine.
7) From the first grade upward, every individual should be pro-

vided with a copy of the United States Constitution and the Bill of Rights, and thoroughly indoctrinated with it. This would help people of all ages to spot totalitarian and unconstitutional practices in their incipient stages.

8) Any employer or government official who demands a urine sample from someone should be required to drink the sample after it has been tested. After all, one base indecency deserves another.

What are really needed are laws to govern the governors and restrain all holders of government office, up to and including the president. These are the people most in need of serious restraint, as they can't seem to mind their own business and stay out of the other people's business.

It is up to those of us who believe in freedom and liberty to preserve that freedom and liberty by foiling the attempts of those who would steal that freedom and liberty from us.

I would like to close this book with three quotations from Thomas Jefferson.

First: "Our liberty depends on freedom of the press, and that cannot be limited without being lost."[1]

Second: "The spirit of resistance to government is so valuable on certain occasions that I wish it to be always kept alive. It will often be exercised when wrong, but better so than not to be exercised at all."[2]

Finally: "God forbid we should ever be twenty years without such a rebellion."

What country ever existed a century and a half without a rebellion?

And what country can preserve its liberties, if its rulers are not warned from time to time, that his people preserve the spirit of resistance. Let them take arms."[3]

NOTES

1. George Seldes, *The Great Thoughts*, 208.
2. Ibid., 208.
3. Ibid., 209.